'Remember When'...

...A STORY OF LIFE, DEATH, LOVE AND FAITH

Jean Witte

WESTBOW
PRESS®
A DIVISION OF THOMAS NELSON
& ZONDERVAN

WestBow Press books may be ordered through booksellers or by contacting:

WestBow Press
A Division of Thomas Nelson & Zondervan
1663 Liberty Drive
Bloomington, IN 47403
www.westbowpress.com
844-714-3454

Because of the dynamic nature of the Internet, any web addresses or links contained in this book may have changed since publication and may no longer be valid. The views expressed in this work are solely those of the author and do not necessarily reflect the views of the publisher, and the publisher hereby disclaims any responsibility for them.

Any people depicted in stock imagery provided by Getty Images are models, and such images are being used for illustrative purposes only.
Certain stock imagery © Getty Images.

ISBN: 979-8-3850-1933-5 (sc)
ISBN: 979-8-3850-1934-2 (e)

Print information available on the last page.

WestBow Press rev. date: 04/15/2024

Contents

Dedication

T his book is dedicated to my children, grandchildren and great grandchildren, but especially to my great granddaughter, Kyla Epple, who was my inspiration when one day she asked me what a telephone was. I immediately began to think about the hand-held devices this generation has become so used to. But this book is not entirely about telephones, but in my 87 years of life on this planet, I have experienced things that this generation would probably never know about had I not taken the time to tell them. Thus, I decided to write it down so each of them could be reminded of a time that was and will never be again.

Foreword

When the thoughts started coming for the story, I know that I had to have a partner in my writing, so I called on God to guide me to do my best with what talent He had given me. So God and I embarked on this venture that I thought would just include my family. The more I wrote, the more things came to mind, and I allowed a few people, including one publisher, to review what I had written. The response was always: 'You should definitely get this published.' So anybody who wants to wander through life with me will be welcome to do so. You may learn more about me than you wish to know, or, hopefully, you will only wish you had been there with me.

I also want to give a special thanks to Kyla's sister, another great granddaughter, Katie Epple, for providing some great and memorable pictures as my daughter, Sarah, my granddaughter Elana Epple, mother of these two granddaughters, Katie and Kyla, and I traveled back in time to my home town of Scottsville, KY. We were able to see so many of my memories and especially the last house my mother and I lived in shortly before her death 79 years ago...what a trip! They were even able to go to the cemetery where my mother and father are buried, and the girls placed flowers on the graves of their ancestor's!

This book is filled with true stories of things that happened in my life and the people I knew along the way. These are stories of joy, sorrow, laughter, tears, the good, the bad and the ugly, as well as some information. But most of all it is written for enjoyment as we spend some time "Remembering When..."

Dear God;

Good morning and thank you for a good night's rest, and to be awakened to your beautiful creation. For there is none like it! As I prepare for my day, I realize that what I need to do besides offering my thanks to you is to ask what I can do for you? That is the way my day should be filled…filled with things you want me to do for you and for your glory.

I try not to allow the evil in this world to effect my attitude or wellbeing. Of course, living alone, as I do, I can remain pretty well isolated from much of the evil world. And Lord, it makes me sad that you created a beautiful, clean and pure universe, only to have those whom you created mess it up! I am sure that if it makes me sad, you are not happy with it either.

Sadly, it seems that Satan is having a heyday, because we humans are playing into his hands! We are inundated with lawlessness and immorality being the rule. I just saw a suggestion on my computer that said: "Life is short…have an affair"!

Our political system is in a mess. The rule of law and common sense seems to have no place in our society anymore. Our news reporters don't seem to be able to report the news honestly and fairly, but rather twist and bend their words to fit an agenda of their own, or of the people for whom they work.

As Christians we are fighting back, but in many cases even our best efforts get undermined. Thank you Lord, that I have a church that teaches pure gospel. We have groups that meet regularly to study your Word. And now we are privileged to have leaders, mostly moms, who are working with a program called "Pearls of Purity", that teaches middle school aged girls to treat their bodies as a temple of God's creation and how to live good moral lives. I have been told that soon there will be a similar program for young boys. How great is this? If these young ones are trained to live right perhaps we will have more families staying together, praying and working to serve the Lord. If these young ones give their hearts and lives to you then they will become good parents who can train their own generations to be godly in an ungodly world.

But I know that you know all this, Lord, and are waiting to deal with the world on your timing. In the meantime may you equip we Christians to be bold and strong in our faith as we wait; for we are weak but You, oh Lord are strong...Come, Lord Jesus, come quickly!

In your precious holy name I pray. Amen

Remember When...

A STORY OF LIFE, DEATH, LOVE AND FAITH

D id I ever tell you about the time when I was a little girl... about 5 years old? I went to visit my Aunt Nellie Howell...my mother's sister. She and her husband, Uncle Porter lived out in the country about 2 or 3 miles from the town of Scottsville, KY, where I was born. I loved to go visit my aunts and other relatives because they thought I was the sweetest little thing to ever come around!

Well, there are many things that I intend to write you about my relatives, but this one came to mind first. Do you really know where eggs come from?? Well, when I was growing up we had to depend on the chickens that were in a pen. There were little boxes or nests hanging outside the coop, as it was called. These little boxes were where the chickens laid their eggs and it made it easier for folks to gather the eggs. The number of eggs in the nest depended first on the number of laying hens one had and second the ability of a particular chicken to produce an egg. Now this process is a strange one and may even alter your feelings about eggs...do you really want me to tell you how the eggs happen? Maybe another time!

Well, even though my aunts and uncles thought I was about the sweetest little thing that ever happened, I have to admit I did some things that were not quite so sweet, and one involved checking the chicken house to see if there were any eggs. Yes, there were several eggs, because the men in the family worked hard and needed to eat a big breakfast so they had lots of eggs. I always wondered if there was a baby chicken inside the egg, so one day I decided to check it out. I cracked one egg...no baby chick...cracked another and no baby chick. After I had broken about 5 or 6 eggs, my aunt came out to see what her sweet little niece was doing. The lesson I learned was to leave the eggs alone and save them for breakfast because cracking them caused my Aunt Nellie to be unhappy and she had to do what Mommies and Daddy's have to do when their sweet little ones do something wrong. Aunt Nellie went to the peach tree that was in her back yard and told me to pick out a little branch, which I did, and she stripped all the leaves off the branch and applied the branch liberally to the backs of my sweet little legs, which stung so bad I wet my pants and promised I would never... EVER crack the eggs again!!

Behind Aunt Nellie's house was a creek. It was so neat. The water was just a little more than ankle deep and I loved to kick and splash and watch the little water bugs that darted around the surface. There was a big tall rock behind the creek and water came down and ran into the creek, making a wonderful relaxing sound. It is a good thing the water wasn't very deep because cars that came by had to drive through the water, there was no bridge. I loved to see car's splash through the water. One day my 3 year old niece was with me and her mother (my sister) let her go with me to the creek but she told her little daughter not to get her clothes wet...but guess what...it wasn't any time until she just sat right down in the water and soaked her clothes. She cried because she knew her mommy would be unhappy. But it wasn't that bad. Mom realized it was an accident and joined in the laughter.

This incident reminds me of something my dear Aunt Ruby said one day. Aunt Ruby was the wife of my daddy's brother Earl Barger, and she was always free, if not a bit off base, with her advice. And this is what she said to her children one day as they headed for the lake... her advice: "Now don't you kids go in that water till you learn how to swim!" How's that for rational thinking? Not too unlike my sister's advice to her little one in allowing her to play in the creek, but to not get her clothes wet! Oh! Well, Mama's do mean well.

Uncle Porter, Aunt Nellie's' husband had a smoke house out in the back yard where they kept meat like ham and such. On the back porch there was a hole in the flooring that had a long metal pipe that went down into the hole and we could draw up water from the well, or cistern. The water was always cold and good. We could also store things like milk and butter down in this hole. I don't remember exactly how that was done, but I remember seeing them pull the other foods out of the well on a box like thing. We did not have a faucet or sink in the house, so this is how we got the water to drink and to cook with. Another thing we didn't have was a bathroom…at least not like what we have in our houses today anyway. No. The bath room was a little building out in the back yard someplace and I used to be afraid to go in there and sit down, because I thought bugs, and spiders and heaven knows what else would come up and bite me. But that was the way it was when I was a little girl…a long time ago. There was no 'Charmin' to take with us. We used the Sears Roebuck catalog!!! Sometimes these little backyard 'bathrooms' were enlarged according to the size of the family. Some were little houses with 2 holes, and one of my relatives who had a large family, even had one with 4 holes…better known as 'The Conference Room'!! There were no secrets in situations like this…it was all in the family, or maybe even a few close friends.

One of my favorite times was bedtime. I started thinking about them a few nights ago as I crawled into bed on my nice Tempurpedic matteress and I remembered that my relatives did not have a nice mattress like mine. No. Their mattress was straw, stuffed into a pouch that the women would make. And I started thinking about how this was done. I loved to crawl in bed and smell the fresh straw. Then I thought about how they could get a cover for the straw. They didn't have sheets like we have now. They bought fabric from a peddler. Now that is something I bet you do not know about. But when I was a little girl, women didn't drive a car, and most families didn't even have a car. They had a horse and carriage, or just plain wagon! Some had a car or a pick-up truck, and the country folk had to wait for the peddler to come around. The peddler would load up his wagon and his horse would pull him around through the countryside and sell items to the families that had no other way of buying things. And it seemed the peddler had EVERYTHING in his wagon. This is how the women got the fabric to make the pouch that held the straw for their mattress. The women often would also make pillow cases and then take the time to embroider pretty designs on the ends just for a nice touch. From this peddler one could purchase most any kind of ingredients for spicing up cooking as well as bottled sure fire pain remedies. Those were the days!!

When I was very young, and since my daddy had died when I was a baby and my mamma had to work, I went to nursery school from the time I was 3 years old. The lady who had charge of the school drove her car over town to pick up the children and take them to school. I didn't particularly like going to school, because every Monday morning all of we students would line up for our tablespoon of mineral oil! YUCK! Oh, I didn't mind it sometimes, but there were times I would just rather stay home and play with my dolls, so guess what I did? I would hide from Mrs. Garrison, the teacher. I say I would hide, but evidently I didn't do a very good job of hiding, because I would sit under our kitchen table. Can you imagine? This is just a table with four legs and a table cloth on it, but the table cloth didn't come down far enough to cover me. I guess I didn't realize that, because I truly thought I was well hidden from Mrs. Garrison. Imagine that...she found me, and I had to go to school. Funny thing is that when I did go to school, I really liked it. I had many friends and we had a really good time, so I don't know why I thought I should hide. As I said I started school when I was 3 years old and felt like I went to school all my life and when I got older and was in high school, I thought I would NEVER get out of school. But I did!

I had two brothers that were older than me. One was 11 years older and his name was Harvle, the other brother was 8 years older than me and his name was Eutra. I also had a sister who was 15 years older than me and she was married and lived in Florida, and had a little girl of her own. My sister's name was Dorothy and her husband was Carl and their little girl was named Patty. I loved all of them very much.

Meet my mother's family
#1 Mother's entire family: Grand Pa and Grand Ma Dalton (seated)
Standing from left: Uncle Joe, Aunt Betty, Uncle Alfred, Uncle Ed,
my mother, Gertie, Aunt Nellie, and Uncle Roy (in the 1930's)

My brothers were at home with my Mamma and me and one day I was playing in a field next to our house and tripped in a hole and fell. When I got up I looked back at the hole and there were 3 baby bunnies in the hole. If you have ever seen a baby bunny you will know just how cute they are. I didn't give a thought to the fact that if I took one out of the hole that their mamma would miss him and she would probably cry and maybe even go looking for her lost baby. So I took a cute, cuddly baby bunny home with me and my brothers built a little cage for the bunny to stay in. Sometimes my mother would let me let the bunny out of the cage and I would play with him on the kitchen floor, but she didn't like it when the bunny decided to pee on the floor, so I had to put him back in the cage. After a while I decided maybe I should take the baby back to his mother. She surely had missed him. So I returned him to his home and smiled a bit, feeling I had definitely done the right thing.

Like I said earlier, my aunts and uncles thought I was the sweetest thing they knew, but I must confess I did get into mischief sometimes. One time I remember was one day after school and one of my friends came home with me. We would play together until it was time for me to walk up town where I would meet my mamma when she got off work and she and I would walk home together. Well, this particular day, mamma was not real happy when we got home because when my friend and I were there alone, we were hungry and mother usually kept baked sweet potatoes in the warmer of our stove. So my friend and I were eating our sweet potato and decided it would also be fun to JUMP ON THE BED! Did you ever do that? Well, while we were jumping and eating we were also dropping bits of the sweet potato onto the bed and jumping in it, not necessarily on purpose, but as we jumped up and down we dropped little pieces of the sweet potato onto the bedspread, and we just naturally stepped in those soft orange colored bit of sweet potato. As poor little innocent girls, we didn't think anything about it...but my mamma did...and I got my fanny tanned when she got home and found the mess in her bedspread! Well, it wasn't really my fanny that got tanned. The way my mother would punish me was usually with a little switch which she took from a tree in the yard. It was usually pretty thin and green, which meant it was going to sting like a bee when it hit my poor little legs!! And I would almost pee my pants when she switched me. POOR LITTLE ME! This got to be pretty much the way of my punishment. And it seemed that no matter where we lived, there was a peach tree with little thin limbs! I say 'no matter where we lived', because that is almost a story in itself. For some reason my mother must have loved to move, because in the 8 years I had my mamma before she passed away at age 45, we lived in 8 houses that I can recall! Sometimes I would come home from school, but my home had moved! I actually remember coming from school one day and did not know where my mamma had moved. I often wondered, but never knew exactly *how* she moved because we only had our feet for transportation. Having such a vivid memory of so much at such a young age caused many to question my stories; however, I have been told that deep memories are not uncommon amongst people who have had traumatic experiences. And I certainly had the experiences, I just don't want to tell them in this book, but I may tell you some other time since there were many and lasted for years. I may do another book about these, because I wanted this to be a happier book.

By the time I was in the second grade, we found out that I was quite musical. We had a band that consisted of kazoos, cymbals, drums and sand blocks. I, being very talented, played the sand blocks. We even had uniforms that my Aunt Mamie made. They were navy blue with gold epaulets. Now, I am not sure about the name or the spelling, but they were like little gold pads with gold fringe on them and they were on the shoulder of the uniform. We were really cute. And believe it or not, as I am writing this, I am 80+ years old, and this was when I was only 7. And many years later, I found out that one of my classmates from Scottsville, KY, who was also in the band, was married and lived in Evansville, IN. I lived in Dale, IN. I called her one day and we were talking about those wonderful days when we were 7 years old, and she told me that her mother had pictures of us in our band uniforms and she would get them if she could. But sadly, her mother passed away before we got the pictures and I didn't talk to Betty Ann anymore because, sadly, again, I read in the paper that she, too, had passed away. It would have been great to have been able to see those pictures. Interestingly, those of us who had the good fortune of having been born south of the Ohio River went by our first two names. When I called to talk to Betty Ann, she laughed and said she knew I had to be someone from her distant past by calling her by both names. She had only been known as Betty when she came to Evansville. But when you cross the Ohio River and go south, you will understand that it is just the way the south works. If your mamma calls you when she is upset, I bet she calls you by your first and second name. But not where I came from! No Indeed! Down South you got the whole name, no matter how long or how eccentric your name might be, if you were in trouble you *knew* what was coming!

As I said before, I wasn't always the perfect little angel that people and family claimed, so I might as well tell you about a fib I told one day.

I was still living at the house where I found the baby bunny, and one day I walked across that field and just across the road was a sweet little lady who also thought I was cute and sweet. After all I was only 5 years old at the time. Her name was Mrs. Campbell, but we lovingly called her 'Granny' Campbell. I spoke to her across the road, and for some reason, I decided to tell her that it was my birthday. Little did she know that while this was May, my birthday wasn't really until September... shame on me! I really didn't give it any more thought until later that afternoon, someone knocked at our back door and when my mamma answered it, there was a delivery boy from the grocery store and guess what he had!! There was a nice big box which had several nice things that we could eat, but there was also a CAKE. It didn't have 'happy birthday' on it or anything like that, but there might as well have been because there was a sweet note from Granny Campbell, wishing me a very happy birthday!

OH, BOY!! My mamma never, ever let me get away with a fib, so I had to go to Mrs. Campbell's house...all by myself...and tell her that I had told her a fib.

You are not supposed to be rewarded for fibbing, but this lady was so sweet, she simply hugged me and told me she loved me anyway and forgave me and hoped that I enjoyed the cake. But I wasn't real sure I could enjoy it after having to confess my sin! Well, I ate it anyway, and the fib I told that sweet little lady has never left my mind!

Everybody in our small town knew me and there was hardly a home in the entire town where I was not welcome to visit. Since my daddy had died when I was a baby and my mamma had the job of raising my two brothers and me, I often would just wander around town after school until about 4:00 pm, when my mother would get off work. She worked in a sewing factory, where they made men's overalls, and I would stand at the door where she came out and we would walk home together. My mother was just about the most precious person I could think of in my life, and we had some great talks on our way home. She also knew that if I was not there to meet her that I would find my way home soon from some other home where I visited. I often went to my Aunt Mamie's house. She and my Uncle Roy lived in a house up on a hill that was known in the town as "Vinegar Hill". I have no idea where the name came from, but people often have certain names for places they want to identify. I spent about as much time with Aunt Mamie as anybody else. One reason was that she had a daughter who was a year older than me and we were very close cousins. As a matter of fact she now lives in Medford, Oregon, and we still keep in touch. We had many great times together. Another reason for loving it at Aunt Mamie's was that she was one of the best cooks around, and I could always count on something good to eat when Margie, my cousin and I, would come home from school. I even spent many nights with them, too. Aunt Mamie's husband was a brother to my father, his name was Uncle Roy, and he looked a lot like my father, so I was told. And since I never got to know my father, it was nice to be able to be reminded of what he might have looked like.

Now on my mamma's side of the family there were several aunts and uncles. One was my Aunt Bettie, who was the one who loved to tuck me in her bed, along with Uncle John and the sweet smelling straw mattress. Also she told me a story one time about when my Grandpa Bill, (on my daddy's side) came to visit her and sat down at her kitchen table where she always had some homemade bread, fresh churned butter and homemade jam. Well, Pa Bill, as I called him, was talking to Aunt Bettie and took a bite of his freshly buttered bread that he had topped with her homemade jam. He remarked to Aunt Bettie that she must have forgotten some seeds in the jam. She was sure that could not be, so she checked it out, only to find that what Pa Bill had thought were seeds, were indeed, large ANTS! They both got a good laugh out of it, and I always thought that was a funny, funny story, but hoped it never happened to me.

Grandpa Bill

Speaking of my Pa Bill, I dearly loved that man!! He lived out in the country and I lived in town. Every day, at least that the weather permitted, Pa Bill would walk into town to visit us and his sister, whose name was Aunt Fletcher Douglas. That was another pretty funny name, but there are a lot of funny names in my family, but the people are great! Although Aunt Fletcher was just a great-aunt, I visited with her often, too. But back to Pa Bill: Another thing Pa Bill never failed to do was to give me a penny or two. Back then I could go to the dime store and find *something*. One day he gave me 11 cents. I hardly knew what to do. I was only 7 years old, and 11 cents was a lot of money. But then I remembered that I had seen a set of gardening tools which I thought would be great for my back yard. So the money didn't stay in my little hands for long and soon I was back home with a wonderful purchase of a rake, a hoe and a shovel, and happy as the little bugs I would probably uncover when I started digging!

What a wonderful man, my Pa Bill! Later after I had moved to Florida, I usually went back to Kentucky every summer and never failed to see Pa Bill. Then one day I got a letter from one of my cousins and he had sent me some pictures of the place where Pa Bill had been buried. I was very, very sad, because no one had told me he was sick, or that they thought he might not live long, and I cried so hard because I didn't get to tell him good bye. But I look forward to the day I will get to see him again when I get to heaven and we can all be together.

Return to church where baptized at age 5

I know I am going to heaven because one Sunday when I was in church, and only 5 years old, I was sitting at the end of one of the church pews, listening to the minister's sermon. My mamma usually came to church with me, but often it was necessary for her to stay home and catch up on some of her house work. We belonged to the First Methodist Church in Scottsville, but she was not with me this particular Sunday. But I was certainly sitting on the edge of my seat listening to our pastor. At the end of his sermon, he started talking about the baptism service that would take place at Trammel Creek that very afternoon and he wanted people who wanted to be baptized to let him know. Otherwise, if there were some who could not go to the creek, he would hold a service right there at the altar. In my very, very young years, I always felt that I knew God was someone special. At this particular moment, while still in my seat, there came a beam, of sunlight through the glass window and shone on me somewhat like a spotlight and I felt a strong pull to go to the altar. I went up, knelt down and I don't remember what the pastor said to me, but I knew this was what I wanted to do, and he blessed me, said some Scripture over me and sprinkled me with the baptismal water. This was a beautiful bright day, I believe it was in May or early June and I didn't live very far from the church and I danced and sang all the way home. I couldn't wait to tell my mamma what had happened. She was thrilled, because all of our family had been strong believers in the Lord and I will tell another story later about a memory I have of my mamma reading her Bible. I have always been grateful that God had me placed in such a family. From that moment on there have been so many times I could not even begin to tell you where God has helped me through problems, sickness, sorrow and most any kind of trouble that might come along. And He also rejoices with me when life was going great, even with the out and out miracles, which I will also tell later. God is great! As a side note, I will also tell you that I did not always attend services at The Methodist Church. There were several different denominations represented in our little town and it was nothing for me to attend a different church each Sunday. No. We didn't have 52 churches, but the ones we had I visited frequently. I finally came to one conclusion: I am a Baptist in my heart and soul! Of all the churches I have attended, I felt that the Baptist preached what I could understand best and meant the most in my developing years as a Christian.

I have to give credit to that thought to reiterate, I say that I am Baptist at heart, and Southern Baptist at that!

Now, while I am thinking about it I will tell you a story about my Uncle Joe. Uncle Joe was one of my mamma's four brothers. He was the only one in our family in town who had a car. I always liked it when he took mamma and me someplace, except I usually got car-sick and they had to stop along the road and let me throw up...then back for the rest of the journey...usually to Edmonton, KY., where Uncle Alfred lived. He was also a brother to my mamma and he ran a funeral home in Edmonton. It was a great big white house and Uncle Alfred had sons, Harold, Carl, Aubrey, Noel and one daughter, Lafell! Those wacky boy cousins of mine just loved to scare the living daylights out of me by threatening to put me in one of the caskets that were kept on the upper floor of their home. They never did, but they loved to tease, especially Noel. Uncle Alfred and Aunt Effie also had one daughter, Lafell, who became one of my dearest cousins. She and her husband lived in Florence, KY and later, in my grown up years, it was nothing for Lafell and me to spend 45 minutes to an hour on the phone. I always felt so bad for her because she had arthritis really bad but no one could tell by the way we talked and laughed on the phone. She passed away several years ago...another of my family I expect to be reunited with in heaven.

I had so much fun when I was a kid, because we had so many relatives in so many places and many different things to do and we visited a lot. All of my family loved to sing good old Gospel music, and not much time elapsed between the time the group got into someone's house and someone was at the piano and the rest of us were singing, and singing!

Anyway, back to Uncle Joe who had the car and also had a cow that he kept on a lot that was almost in town. Scottsville was a very small town, probably about the size of Dale, maybe 900 people. Often around 4:30 or 5pm, Uncle Joe would drive down to milk the cow and quite often he stopped for me to go with him. He would get one pail of milk, and carry it back home for his wife, Aunt Nora, to churn into butter. She would skim the butter off and then there was some wonderful butter milk with bits of butter in it, and fresh butter, and sweet milk as well.

Poor ole Aunt Nora, she dipped snuff! If you don't know what that is, it is crumbles of tobacco that people would take a pinch of and place in the lower part of their mouth between the gums and lower teeth. It was a very nasty habit, but Aunt Nora had it. It was so funny when she churned because she had a rhythm with her left foot and the screened door. She would work the handle of the churn up and down, and when her snuff had gotten pretty liquid, she would have to spit it out, and she would push the door open with her left foot and spit through the opening of the door. I don't think she ever missed, and it was funny to watch.

Don't know if you have ever seen a butter churn, but they come in different styles, and sizes, the one Aunt Nora had was a wooden one that stood about 2 and a half feet off the floor and had a long stick that went into a hole in the lid on the wooden churn. She would have to plunge that stick up and down until she knew when the butter was ready to be removed. Thank goodness she never got any of that nasty snuff into the butter or the milk. She could also make buttermilk out of this process, too, but there had to be a 'starter' in order to make the sweet milk sour, just the right amount. I loved buttermilk, and still do. Many people do not. But the buttermilk that came from this process tasted better than any I have ever been able to taste since way back then! Also, there is no comparison between the butter you buy at the store and what we got out of that milk that especially came fresh from Uncle Joe's cow!

There was another fun filled incident with Aunt Nora that I can't forget! I was at her house a lot also, while waiting for mother to get off work, or sometimes if I was sick and couldn't go to school. I have forgotten this particular reason why I was not in school, but I was staying with Aunt Nora this one day. Evidently I did something that caused Aunt Nora to decide to punish me by making me sit in a chair in the middle of the room, so she could keep an eye on me all the time... now why would she do that??? Wasn't I the sweetest kid in the family, or even the whole wide world?? Oh, well, somehow, I had access to one of those little pistols that has a spring inside the nozzle and a stick with a rubber suction cup thingy on the end of it. You push the stick into the end of the pistol and aim it at a target that came with the game and the closer you got to the center, the better your score. So I was playing with this while waiting for my punishment to end. Then I saw a wonderful opportunity...Aunt Nora leaned over to take something out of the oven, and I took advantage of the NEW target!! Good one!! Well at least it was fun, but I ended up with a few stripes on the back of my legs from the little switch I had become pretty used to. I guess she had a peach tree in her backyard, too!

Just down the street from Aunt Nora and Uncle Joe was one of my favorite places to visit. It was the home of Mrs. Cora Huntsman and she had several fish ponds in her back yard. She also had beautiful flowers scattered around and a few little concrete statues of a little girl watering the flowers, or a little boy picking some. One of the most popular stone statues of that era was a little black boy holding a lantern. Of course, over the years, there has been so much sensitivity about black people that no one ever has any of those anymore. I couldn't even tell you how many different kinds and colors of fish were in her ponds. I was always fascinated by all of them. Sometimes she would let me feed them.

Then I had another lady friend down the street from me, I can't remember her name, now, but on a hot summer day she would call me over and let me stand under her garden hose as she watered her flowers. She had more beautiful flowers than Mrs. Huntsman had fish.

Another thing I did for entertainment was roller skate. I loved to skate, and do you know that I never ever learned how to skate backwards. We had a roller rink in town and somehow I always got to skate for free! People just new our circumstances and they took care of me. How fortunate I have always been!

I also remember a Christmas gift that I loved so much that I cried. We were very, very poor and although I was rich with friends and things to do, I didn't often get much that was bought. Well, this wasn't really bought, either. Our town had a Christmas party downtown in the great big courthouse building. I always liked to go in there because usually when you talked very loud, you could hear the echo...always fascinating to a 5 or 6 year old. Well, this one Christmas my mamma and brothers took me to the courthouse for the Christmas party. We were given sacks of candy; saw Santa Claus, who handed out special gifts. I have no idea what any other child got, all I know is that I was given the cutest little baby doll and a doll bed to boot!! I could not have been happier. Later, I found out that it had belonged to another little girl who had out grown it and wanted to give it to someone else. Her name was Billie Jo Pitchford. Forever after that I thought she was about the sweetest girl I knew. It has always reminded me of how happy someone else can be with something they no longer need and are willing to pass it on rather than throw it away. You never know when you are going to make someone else very happy...just like me!

Before I forget, I wanted to tell you about one of my favorite pastimes in the summer. It just seemed like there could be nothing more fun than lying on your back on the side of a little hill and looking up into the sky and making pictures out of the cloud formations. I found everything from puppies, to a field of sheep, in which I always thought Jesus must be close by guarding His sheep. I have seen whales, boats, all kinds of animals and passed many hours just looking into the sky...then along with that we would quench our thirst by getting a bottle of cola and dropping salted peanuts in to it. What a treat! It was just a bunch of kids wandering around town looking for something to do and finding treasures every place we looked. There were usually 3 or 4 of us making a lifetime of memories.

My brothers were very creative too, and they loved to fly kites, and I loved to help them make their kites as well as fly them. We had to make our own kites, so the boys would get some small sticks that could make a good cross piece. They would then tie it together with string. When they had this base for it, they would get an old newspaper and fit it around the sticks to shape the kite. They made the glue to hold the paper on the frame out of flour and water. I'm not real sure how it worked, but it did. When they finished that, they would have mamma get them some strips of rags and tie them together to make the tail of the kite. Next they found all the cotton string they could and rolled it in a figure '8' around another small stick so they could release whatever amount of string they needed. It was quite primitive, but it worked and we had fun doing it. At least my brothers let me help them with some of their projects...they were pretty good guys...I loved them so much!

(pic #24)

I have a very sad story about my brother Eutra. When he grew up he was so smart that every job he was hired to do soon took him up the ladder, fast. I was so proud of him. He got married and had a little girl also named Vickie, almost like my own Vikki. But that marriage didn't work out and I lost contact with his Vickie for several years. Eutra eventually married again to lady named Barb. Together they had a son named Jeff. This has become one of the hardest things for me to deal with, but in the end it has had a marvelous ending!! Eutra and Barb separated and he lived in Clearwater, while Barb chose to stay in Indiana. Things happen in life that just cannot be fully understood and this was a major one for me. As I have said, Eutra's nickname was 'Chigger', and he loved to drink, and did so excessively, and his drinking problem often led to fights and many things I have never really known about, nor do I want to know. But life must have become something Eutra could not deal with. He had lost his joy in life and would try to drown his problems by drinking. He was living alone in a trailer park, far from what he could have been and I don't have any answers to the question as to why one day, or maybe night, life became too much for Chigger so he took his revolver and ended what could have been a good life. This was in January, 1961 when he was not quite 37 years old, and as I write this, the pain is still there. What happens to anyone who loses such a grip on life that they have to end it?? A question I will never have answered.

As sad and painful as this ordeal was, he had left a nine month old son to be raised by his mother. A year or so after Eutra died, Barb married a wonderful man named Ralph Spalding. Ralph had no sons and he gladly adopted Jeff and raised him as his own. Another sad twist to this story is that when Jeff was only 14 years old, his mother died of cancer. Ralph cared enough for his adopted son, and he became a wonderful role model for Jeff. I didn't have much close contact with Jeff for several years, but when I did, we became bonded immediately. As fate would have it, shortly after Jeff was about 22, Ralph died. It did not take long for Jeff and I to become closer. So, as sad as this story is, the rest of the story is wonderful. Gail and I had only one son, and I miscarried a baby boy sometime along the way, and Jeff, not having any other living relative, except his half- sister Vickie, with whom he never had any sort of relationship, I was there with open arms and a happy heart, feeling I had the second son I had always wanted. Jeff and I are as close as mother and son. I don't get to see him often, but we know even though he lives in Indianapolis and I in Evansville, our hearts are connected, and my family has taken Jeff in as a brother.

Jeff & Betsy

Life often seems to betray us when we are happy and enjoy life, and it was no different with Jeff. At this point, Jeff and Betsy, his first wife, were still together when we got the news that Jeff was having major problems with his heart. His story was such that it made the newspaper.

In the fall of 1991, Jeff felt a bit under the weather, and thought he had the flu. He checked himself into the IU medical center on March 25, just a few days after his 31st birthday on March 13th, and the news he got from the doctor caught him completely off guard. He told me later that he called Betsy to let her know where he was and his room number, and that is the last memory he has of an unbelievable story, at least for the next 5 days. It seems it was much more than the flu; Jeff had a heart that was almost like mush, and during that 5 day period he had undergone 3 open heart surgeries and was literally at death's door!

As things like this usually go, it is those who are waiting with all the support system they can find and all the prayers that can be prayed, while the patient in unaware of what his body is going through. All of this was just a big story to Jeff because he only knew what he was told, and it was difficult for him to believe such a story could really have been taking place in his body. Rarely was there a time when the doctors came to report to Betsy and her family that gave any hope at all for Jeff's recovery. It seems that the word 'death' was heard more than any other... and the only alternative! As Jeff recalled later, the medical term for his problem was acute cardiomyopathy, or irregular heartbeat brought on by viral myocarditis, a rare heart infection. Ironically, according to Jeff's recollection of what the doctor told him, the antibodies produced by his immune system to fight the virus worked to destroy the very muscle they were trying to save.

On Thursday night that week Jeff's heart stopped beating. The amazing medical team was determined to save this young man's life, no matter how hard his body worked against them. So they re-split his previously opened sternum and massaged his heart by hand to keep him alive. At one point it is said that one of the doctors remarked that Jeff was still alive only by the Grace of God! People as sick as Jeff usually do not live more than a couple of days. There must be a reason Jeff was still alive!

To assist the failing organ while waiting for the new one, doctors put a left ventricular assist device, leaving a 95% chance he would need a transplant. His condition improved slightly, but it was enough to give a beam of hope. There was some more bad news...that new heart had better be available soon! The doctors decided to install the right side of the make-believe heart when miracle of miracles, the doctors detected Jeff's heart improve on its own! At this point they left Jeff in the operating room with his chest OPEN to observe and wait!! He stayed there all day Friday! Jeff miraculously improved on his own. Then we have another miracle! Jeff was well enough to be sent home without a transplant. The size of the respirator that was used damaged his voice box, and I recall the first time I talked with him on the phone, it was difficult for me to understand him clearly. I made it clear to him that I did not want him to do any further damage to his voice and I would wait until I could see him and maybe we could pass notes. But we could tell from the stories he told that he had really been in another world and at times was hallucinating. Then the possibility of permanent brain damage was mentioned...but we didn't want to think about that! Just bask in the fact that his heart was pumping on its own and he was going home!

Betsy did her best to see that he was taken care of and friends and family helped move Jeff's bedroom downstairs so he wouldn't have stairs to climb, and he was outfitted with a new color TV. So after having entered the hospital on March 25th, he went home on April 12, but remained on the heart transplant list, and carried his phone with him at all times, because he never knew when the call would come, and he wanted to be ready to get a new heart. Sarah and I went to Indy to visit him as soon as we could after he got home. We were so encouraged by his up-beat attitude, which we felt certain was a big part of the battle!

And right now I have forgotten the evening it happened, but my phone rang in Dale, IN...it was Jeff! He and Betsy had been out to dinner when the call came and he wanted to let me know it was time! I told him that Gail and I would be there as soon as we could get there... Jeff was about to receive his new heart!!!

We drove to Indy that night and went to the hospital early the next morning...Betsy and her family were there, and Jeff was in surgery. So here we are again, the ones on the outside pacing the floor and praying while the patient sleeps. I don't remember exactly how long it was, but it seemed forever before the nurse came to tell us we could see him! What? See him already!! Wow!! We gave Betsy first chance to see her husband, hopefully regaining a brand new life.

When the nurse said I could see him, I could hardly contain my joy. But I didn't expect what I saw! I was reassured by the nurse that by simply putting on a mask, I could open the door to his room and say 'Hi'! I really wanted to give him a great big hug, but knew that would have to come later. So I opened the door and there is my precious nephew in a bed with a room full of, for better words...contraptions...I have never seen so many tubes and 'stuff' to sustain one person. And this is what this guy said to me: "Hi, Aunt Jean...I've had a change of heart!" What an understatement!! I could no longer hold back the tears of joy!

But we also knew he was just at the beginning of a lengthy recovery and adjustment to his new heart, which we learned could probably have come from a seventeen year old young man who had died in an automobile accident!

That was thirty one years ago and although he needs special medication, Jeff is healthy and enjoying helping to raise his 15 year old daughter. He and second wife Lisa, sadly divorced, and that always creates difficulty for the entire family. Jeff and Lisa have differing ideas on parenting, and though I do not know how Lisa disciplines Elly, I do know that Jeff is a model father, teaching and modeling a very practical life for his daughter. We enjoy seeing them whenever possible and thank God every day for another of His miracles!

God is so good!!!

Lick your finger...turn the page and get ready for a totally different story...I can shift gears in a heartbeat!!

I have another kite story that maybe one for the records. I was living in Clearwater, FL and probably 10 or 12 years old and I, like my brothers, loved to fly kites and did so many times. But one evening my friend Mary Helen and I readied our kite for launching from my cousins front yard where we had no problem with wires of any kind or anything else that should hinder a wonderful adventure. Little did we know at the onset just how wonderful and exciting it would become. It seemed the wind was perfect and we got our kite off the ground and sailing beautifully in the early evening sky. Up, up, and away it went until we were getting low on string, and our beautiful kite was asking for more. Mary Helen's grandmother had a fish market just across the highway from where we were. Since Mary Helen knew her grandmother had a good supply of string in her market place, we could easily be given a big reel of string, surely enough to satisfy our kite which seemed to be enjoying its trip to the moon...so we fed it! The kite kept climbing and soon we were attracting the neighbors who wanted to see just how far this kite could go. Again we ran out of string and Mary Helen went once more to her grandmother, and again we fed this hungry kite more string. It began getting late and the kite was almost out of sight, but we went on as long as we felt we could, because bringing that kite in just might be an ordeal in itself, So we started winding in the string and trying to guide our out of sight kite. Soon we saw it and had the feeling the kite wasn't ready to leave its lofty heights, but we felt we must, and we did, carefully guiding it into the safety of our yard. What we found sort of amazed us. We had no idea just how high that kite had flown, but when we retrieved it, we were aware that although there was no moisture on the ground where we were, the kite was so wet we thought it should not even be able to fly...but it did, and we will always have that memory of one very special kite and often wished for the same atmospheric conditions to launch another, but it never happened.

Remember I said I would tell you more about my mamma reading her Bible. I don't know if she had one before, but one year for Christmas, her boss at the factory where she worked gave every worker a Bible. And I have kept this Bible and had it recovered and placed my mamma's name along with the name of my oldest great-granddaughter, Katie Epple, and gave it to her because she had expressed to her mother the desire to have it. I also included a paper with the names of all my family members, and anything of importance I could remember. It is comforting to me to know that this piece of my life will go on. But the time my mamma received this Bible was also a time when we did not have electricity, so every night, I remember her sitting in her wicker rocking chair reading her Bible by the light from a kerosene lamp. The wicker chair that she sat in is still, hopefully in the family. It was the first furniture I remember in our house. A cousin bought it when mother and I were getting ready to move to Florida when I was 8 years old. He used it in the waiting room of his photography studio. One day, many years later, he called me and said he was redecorating his waiting room and asked if I wanted this chair and the 3-piece settee that went with it. This was after I was married and living in Indiana with my husband and 3 children. YES!! I definitely wanted this furniture! It held so many memories. I kept it at my house for several years, and then Vikki (our oldest) wanted it for her house. She had it refinished and reupholstered and it was quite beautiful. When her life changes made it no longer feasible for her to keep it, she asked if I wanted it back. I really didn't have any place to put it, but I definitely did not want to lose this precious memory. After all it was still in extremely great shape and had been purchased in the1930's. So our daughter Sarah took the furniture for her porch. It should still be in the family and sitting at the home of Justin & Elana, (my granddaughter & husband) who also appreciate the wonderful attachment that I have with it. So Katie or Kyla (their daughters) may someday be able to have it in their home. We will keep it until it falls apart. Every time I see it, I can see my mamma sitting in it reading her Bible by the dim light of a kerosene lamp!

One more thing while I am speaking of my mamma. I think you can tell from this story that I loved my mamma very much. This one is concerning Mother's Day. It was a Saturday night, the night before Mother's Day and my brothers and I were in the front room of our house and I was telling them how I wanted to give mamma something for Mother's Day, but had no money. These two boys, who had very little money, reached into their pockets and came up with something like 10 or 15 cents,. It was all they could find and they gave it to me and I made a mad dash for the dime store down town. When I came back, I was so excited with my purchase I simply could not wait until morning to give it to mamma. I had bought a framed picture for a dime that had the scene of something of a woodsy nature but had the sweetest verse about how much I loved my mother. I gave it to her that very evening and I will never forget how she took me in her arms, hugged and kissed me and cried! Am I fortunate, or what!!??

This is just about the time that things began to change for me because my mother got very sick. I never did know just what was wrong. But my sister, Dorothy who had married Carl Bandy, had moved to Orlando, Fl and wanted mother and me to come down and live with them. My two brothers had gone down several months earlier and Dorothy just wanted us to all be together. Did I mention any place before that I loved my sister just about as much as I loved my mother? She was 15 years older than me, and I remember how she hated to leave whenever they came to visit.

Mamma decided this was what we should do and she thought it best to just sell everything we had, except for our clothes, (and my mamma's Bible), and make the change. That is when she got sick. My great aunt Fletcher Douglas lived next door to us, so mamma went to her house until all of our belongings sold. It was done by auction. This is where my cousin Aubrey Dalton, bought the wicker furniture that I mentioned earlier that ended up with my mother's great- grand daughter Elana's house, so Katie and Kyla, two of *my* great grand-daughters were able to use the very furniture that my mamma and I had for our living room furniture.

We did not have very many possessions to sell at the auction. I remember the bed mamma and I slept in and a bed the boys had, a wooden table with four chairs, a dresser, and the wicker furniture. The only valuable thing, at least to me that I remember having to sell was my roller skates. That was my real pass time. I loved to roller skate. I guess she figured I probably would not get to use them where we were going, or maybe we just didn't have room to take them...then again, I'm sure she needed every penny she could get, for we did not have much. But my heart was broken when my treasured roller skates sold for 10 cents!! There would not be sidewalks where we went, so I really had no use for them; nevertheless, my heart was broken!

Mamma was still very sick and Uncle Joe took us out in the country to stay with mamma's sister, my Aunt Nellie… the aunt at whose house I was staying when I decided to check to see if there were any chickens in the eggs. Well, by this time Aunt Nellie had forgiven me and I was 3 years older, and remember they all still thought I was the sweetest child they ever knew!

We arrived at Aunt Nellie's on September 10, 1940.

Days went by and mamma still didn't get any better. The only place we could go to call the doctor was about 2 miles up the road to my Aunt Pearl's house. She and Uncle Ira were the only ones with a telephone for miles around. (Remember, the word 'telephone' is what started my inspiration to write this book, so there will be more about different telephones over the years). Every day Aunt Nellie would write a note for the doctor and I would walk to Aunt Pearl's house and she would call the doctor and I would wait for the message to take back to my Aunt Nellie. I walked this trip almost every day if it wasn't raining, then Uncle Porter would drive me. I always liked to go to Aunt Pearl's even if Uncle Porter could have taken the note, because Aunt Pearl and Uncle Ira had 10 kids…10 kids…all in one family, so I had more than one playmate when I went there. There is more to tell about my visits to Aunt Pearl, but the story about my mamma went on for a few weeks and she never got better.

The trips to Aunt Pearls were usually uneventful and quite often pretty tiring, but that was my job… to help my mamma get better. Then there were the times when two kids who lived in the house my grandma and grandpa Dalton had lived in several years before, and they had a German shepherd dog and would hide in the weeds and when I walked past they would push this big dog into my path. Needless to say, it scared me pretty bad, but I tried to not let them know it bothered me at all.

Now I want to tell you a bit about my grandma and grandpa Dalton before I go on, because I was told years ago that the infamous "Dalton Gang" that wreaked havoc in Kentucky and later joined up with some others and robbed banks, and killed people, was from Logan County, KY and their father was either a brother or some close relation to my grandpa Dalton. Their father's name was Frank Dalton. I was also told that when they were in KY, they would come visit some of my family. One of them was named Uncle Krit, and I was told, my mother was so scared of him she would hide when he came by.

Grandma's name was Nancy Catherine. She was a very small lady with gray hair that she wore in a bun on the top of her head. I remember most of all that she sat in a rocking chair in front of the big open fireplace where she had a big black kettle that hung over the fire and she would usually be cooking something. I was only 4 years old when she died in 1936, but I do have a little memory of her, and then Grandpa, whose name was William Andrew, but was called Willie "Q", for some reason, lived only two more years and I remember him being a pretty big man, but I was just a little girl and he probably wasn't as big as I thought, but to me he looked as big as a mountain, and had the prettiest blue eyes I have ever seen. I am so glad that I got to know them at least for a little while, but I sure didn't care much for the mean kids who lived in their house and had the big dog. And certainly hoped those wild Dalton's were not around anymore. Remember these are YOUR relatives. I am just connecting you to the past in hopes you will enjoy knowing how things were back when I was a child and knew these people personally. (all but the so-called Dalton Gang). I am telling you true stories!!

I made the trips to Aunt Pearl's for many days, and then one afternoon Aunt Nellie and I were in the kitchen shelling lima beans. Aunt Nellie had washed some sheets that day and they were hanging on the clothes line in the back yard. The air was very still, not a breeze blowing at all, when all of a sudden one of the sheets flew up in the air as if a big puff of wind had come along, but there was none. Aunt Nellie put down her pan of beans and left the room to check on mamma, and came back right away and took me in her arms and told me that my mamma had died. She had said that there was an old wives tale that she remembered: 'If a sheet blew up in the breeze when there was no wind, it was a sign of a death.' That is what made her go to check on mamma. I never have really believed in 'Old Wives Tales', but this sure makes you wonder. Losing my mother was one of the hardest things for me to deal with in my life. I didn't know I had so many tears as I shed for days after she died.

1939:
Uncle Ed, Aunt Beulah, 3 years old Patty. Daughter of my
sister Dorothy standing next to mu brother Harvle

My sister Dorothy, husband Carl and my two brothers came up from Florida for the funeral and took me back home with them to start a new life leaving behind someone very precious to all of us. The funeral and burial were at Mt, Pleasant, a neat little church just outside Scottsville, and the place where several of my relatives are buried, including my father and a sister who died before any of the other of we kids were born. And even 'Pa Bill' is buried there. This was not an easy time and to make it even worse, Dorothy was 8 months pregnant with her second child and the trip to mother's funeral was not easy for her. Road conditions and even the cars did not make travelling as easy as it is today. But we made it back to Orlando where Dorothy's family now had increased from just her husband and daughter, to twice as many. Our 2 brothers and I make a full house. But we managed and I remember Dorothy being very happy. That must have been so important to her.

Remember I told you about people using both their first and second names, at least those of us who were born south of the Ohio River. Well, my family's names went like this: Dorothy 'C'...her middle name was Claudia, after our father, Claude. But Dorothy Claudia was a bit much so it was shortened, as was my bother Harvle 'D'. His first name was the same as Pa Bill's first name, and his second name was Dalton, our mother's maiden name. Then came Eutra Lee and Doris Jean. Eutra had a nickname of 'Chigger'. I think that was because he could get under your skin, but everybody loved him anyway. As for me, I went by Doris Jean until I was about 15 when somebody just started calling me Jean, and it seemed to stick...just a bit of history behind our names.

Dorothy and Carl did not have very much room in their modest little home and I had to sleep in the baby crib with Patty who was 3½ years old. I wasn't very big, but that is a lot to put in a baby crib. The house was not very big, just 2 bedrooms, 1 bath a kitchen and small living room for 6 people and most of them grown. But we made it, for a brief time anyway. Then Dorothy got sick and had to go to the hospital. Patty and I were taken to her paternal grand- parents, the Bandy's who ran a newspaper in Orlando. When Dorothy went to the hospital we were hoping things were not serious, but, maybe it was just time for the new baby. But something else was wrong, and I never knew for sure just what it was, but it required that she be in the hospital for a longer time. The Bandy's couldn't take care of me for an extended time so they took me to Clearwater where I had and aunt and uncle. Uncle Ed was one of my mother's brothers and he had lived in Clearwater, Florida for many years...he and my Aunt Beulah. It was nice there and I had a room all to myself, although, I was scared at night and would cry for someone to come and be with me. But remember, I was barely 8 years old, and had just lost my mother and had spent a brief time yet unsettled with my sister, then had to move again. My aunt was good to me and came and would lay with me in bed and tell me everything would be OK.

But I was afraid and felt awfully alone! I missed my mamma and also wanted to be with my sister.

About three weeks after I had come to Clearwater, I heard the phone ring one night. I heard Uncle Ed answer it, but I couldn't hear the conversation. Soon Aunt Beulah came into my room and crawled in bed with me and took me in her arms and told me that my sister had died. Not only that, but the baby had also died. My world was shattered once again. Sure I was sad and heartbroken, but I never remember wondering what would happen to me next. I may have felt lonely and at sometimes even afraid, but this is when I look back over my life and knew God had been taking care of me all along, and I never did worry about anything, like where I would stay, or with whom. God truly did provide for me.

After Dorothy's funeral, my mother's entire family came over to Clearwater. I guess they were going to make the decision as to what would happen to me. I never really heard their conversation, but several years later, Uncle Ed told me that none of them felt like they wanted to take on the responsibility of rearing an 8 year-old, and they decided I should go to an orphanage. But Uncle Ed said, emphatically: "NO"!! He told them in no uncertain terms that he could not let his sister's child go to an orphanage and that he would take the responsibility. He became my legal guardian, and I loved this man and respected him. He was a very honorable man! I lived with Uncle Ed and Aunt Beulah until I was 16 years old. Again, God blessed me with a Christian home and a loving aunt and uncle to take care of me. One of the most beautiful things I remember having been told was that just before Dorothy died, she repeated the 23rd Psalm in its entirety, and had the hospital staff in tears. To me, this is another of those precious memories one could hold forever.

Life in Florida went on much like life back in Kentucky, I just always went to bed wherever I was and ate with whoever prepared the meal and thanked God every day that He was taking care of me. I did really thank God a lot, although it was not always a strong thought it was just a feeling and I knew I was being taken care of.

The first obstacle in Florida was going to school...YUCK! I didn't want to have to go to a school where the only person I knew was my red-headed cousin who lived up the street. She and I had some unpleasant events in our lives mainly that ended up with me feeling bad. I realized years later that the reason Bobbie treated me like an outcast was that I had infringed on her territory without even realizing how it would affect her. See, she was the first granddaughter, and of course, the apple of Mamma and Daddy Dalton's eyes. These are the names she had chosen to call her grandma and grandpa, and for the years I lived with them I called them by the same affectionate names. After I moved away, I returned to calling them Uncle Ed and Aunt Beulah, but while there, it just seemed to make things smoother.

Now, I have always been one who likes to have things running smoothly, but I think my 'sweet cousin' Bobbie really liked to stir the pot, especially if she could do anything to hurt my feelings or my standing with the kids at school. It really was a bummer! We even had some real good knockdown, drag out fights complete with loud words and any physical harm we could get away with. My greatest trophy was a handful of that red hair. One day I remember whatever she had said or done had really ticked me off and resulted in my grabbing a hand full of hair from each side of her head and literally lifting myself off the floor, coming away with enough strands of red hair to make me feel the winner! But she also got her trophy when she deliberately threw a wooden croquet ball to my mouth resulting in a swollen lip and chipped tooth!

We really didn't share much in common, but due to the circumstances, we were forced to live in harmony as best we could. There were very few trips anyplace that she and I didn't end up in a fight in the back seat of the car. Funny thing is as much difference as there was between Bobbie and I, her brother Arnold and I were great buds and still are to this day. Bobbie hasn't spoken to me for several years but we have made pretenses over the years, while deep inside there was this great big 'just get out of my life' feeling!

Arnie as we affectionately call him was one of my best friends, along with a girl who lived 2 doors down from my house, named Mary Helen. The three of us would play Tarzan...climb trees and give the big ole Tarzan call when we were ready for another adventure in the swamp just up from our houses.

And when the Second World War came, there a couple of military air bases around our area, McDill and Drew Air Force bases were just across the Bay in Tampa and with other military stationed in most of the hotels around Clearwater it was nothing to see convoys of military vehicles loaded with soldiers go down the highway, which was just at the end of New York Street where we lived. We were very patriotic, Arnie, and Mary Helen and me...when we knew the trucks were coming by I got my flag, Arnie got a drum and Mary Helen got her baton and we cheered the troops as they went by...boy did we feel patriotic!! The soldiers would call out to us and wave and we felt so proud!

Mary Helen and I 'saved' Arnie's life one day when we were playing in a field that was kind of rough and in Florida it was not difficult to find snakes and things...well, while wandering through the underbrush, we spotted a SNAKE! Now Mary Helen is a year younger than my seven years and Arnie is 6 years younger than me, so by all means, it was our duty to protect this child! We grabbed Arnie and stood him on a tree stump and screamed for help! Neighbors were always home and close by and right away came to our rescue and assured us that we probably saved Arnie's life by our noble deed, although the snake was a little green snake about 8 inches long. To us it might as well have been a cobra or a 10' rattle snake! And we felt we saved his little life. Oh, yeah, we really were great buds and enjoyed many, many wonderful days, swinging from the trees, yelling like Tarzan and anything else we might happen to encounter on any given day! Our imaginations ran wild!

One part of our play time that Arnie didn't participate in was when Mary Helen and I decided to act out the Hawaiian movie we had just seen with Dorothy Lamour and her famous sarong. We didn't have sarongs, but we made Hula skirts from the branches of the big Chinaberry tree that was in our back yard. The tree had pretty purple blooms in April, and those blooms were always used as the sign of the time we could take off our shoes and go bare footed. The fronds from the chinaberry tree were pretty long and leafy and we would gather enough of them to go around our waists and sew them together with a big heavy needle and heavy cotton thread. We used some sort of bright colored material for a top and then added a necklace we made by sewing the green chinaberries together, much like people often sew cranberries together for Christmas decoration. We would sing our own Hawaiian music or find some on the radio and hula, hula, hula!! Fun! Fun! Fun!

So as feminine as were the make believes Mary Helen and I did, Arnie and I loved to do military camps. His dad, Pete Walker, and his mom, Wilma, together built small tents and cots, and sandbags. They bought a whole bunch of metal soldiers and trucks and jeeps and artillery, and whatever it took to make a great army camp. Remember, the time I was living this was during the Second World War, so it was a vital part of our thinking. Often I got up early in the morning, had breakfast and after getting done whatever chores I had to do, I would head up the street to Arnie's house and his mother allowed us to just dump all those military things in the floor of the dining room and we honestly would play until we had to stop for lunch, then come back and play until supper time. That was great fun and great memories.

Since Arnie and I were such good buds, I was asked to entertain him 3 Easter's in a row. One year he had measles, one year mumps and the next, chicken pox, all over Easter weekend! Since I had already had all these, I was given the job of reading and finding some way to keep Arnie from getting bored while the rest of the family attended church...again another group of happy memories. And I always think about how differently 2 children in the same family can be, as a matter of fact, at this writing (2019), I keep in touch with Arnie via email, and he is a strong Christian Conservative, and, you guessed it...Bobbie was a diehard fan of President Obama, who is anything but Conservative, or even good for our country. (My personal opinion and I just had to throw that in!)

At the same time, during the war, when we went to church on Sunday, Aunt Beulah always invited one, two or maybe even three or four soldiers to come to our house for Sunday dinner. There was a bus that brought these soldiers to church and we would take care of them from that point. I was too young to date, so these guys were treated like brothers, especially nice since I had two brothers who were fighting in the war, one in the Pacific Ocean region and the other in Europe. It was just one of those good Christian things that people do, and I certainly had good examples set for me!

There was one very memorable event with Bobbie and Mary Helen and me. Aunt Beulah and Wilma always went grocery shopping on Friday morning and we girls were big enough to be trusted at home... heh..heh...heh...! This particular shopping Friday was overcast and it must have been in the spring, because it was not very hot. I have no recollection of where the idea came from, or who brought it up, but it was OK'd by all three of us...We went to the shed behind Bobbie's house and got one of Bobbie's mother's galvanized wash tubs and decided to take it down into the field across from Bobbie's house to the little creek that we had been told was BOTTOMLESS! But we were adventuresome! Can you imagine 3 girls, probably ages, 9, 10, and 11 off on such a trip? We got the tub into the water and one by one each brave little girl stepped into the tub, silently praying that it didn't tip over, because after all, we had been told that the creek was BOTTOMLESS! ... SUCCESS!! We were afloat! For a few minutes!! The next thing we knew, we were struggling to get to the bank and get out of that bottomless creek. And now we had another problem...our clothes were drenched! How on earth were we going to be able to get those clothes dried before the Mamma's came home? So the wheels of ingenuity started turning and we decided the best thing to do, after we hauled the tub out of the water and back up to the house, was to build a fire and try to dry our clothes *that* way. We had no idea how much time we had before the Mamma's would return and probably skin us alive! We got ourselves pretty well dried and began to feel that we would be sweet little innocent girls with no sign of disobedience! But we forgot one big thing...WE SMELLED LIKE A SMOKE HOUSE!! And the mamma's had no trouble recognizing the aroma! To be honest, I am not certain exactly how the punishment was doled out, but I believe it felt sort of like those little green switches I used to have to pick for my punishment from the peach tree in the back yard, back in Kentucky. Those were the kind of whippings that one remembers forever, because those little switches on those little legs really hurt! It is interesting in that possibly the only thing that Bobbie and I ever did as a team... and look where it got me! Actually she was pretty good at creating situations where she would benefit and I would carry the scars! Oh, well, that's life with some relatives and I really shouldn't hold any of it against her and I have forgiven her for everything except for voting for Obama!!

As to other fun times…music played a very big part in our family. Joys was a gifted musician. Oops, I didn't tell you about Joys, did I? Joys was the other daughter of Uncle Ed and Aunt Beulah. She was single and 21 years old when I came to live with them. She was a couple of years younger than my sister, and having just lost my sister, at age 23, it took no time for Joys and me to become 'sisters', and remained that way as long as she lived. But, as I said she was a gifted musician and could play the organ, guitar, and piano. For a while she played with a group of professional businessmen in a band they called "The Skillet Lickers". The group consisted of Joys on guitar, Burt, the banker, on piano, Doc, the dentist on the violin, Cy, the constable on banjo, and another whose name escapes me, played the mandolin. They were really very good and even performed on the radio several times. Their practices were in our living room. Fun! Fun! Fun! One of the memorable numbers they played featured the Constable, Cy Lowery, who played the banjo and sang "Charmin' Betsy". The unique thing about Cy and his rendition of his song was that he was a gum chewer and before he would sing, he would take the gum out of his mouth and stick it behind his ear until he finished his song.

Another interesting fact about Cy was that he was probably 5' 9" and weighed over 300 lbs. He was quite a sight with his big Stetson hat and his gun belt, complete with gun somewhere around his waist! He was quite a guy.

I just thought of a good one on **me!!** Speaking of Cy Lowery and his banjo reminded me of a song I sang one time that drew some raised eyebrows. I wasn't to blame for the wrong words, after all, I had Uncle Ed as my father figure and I was sure it would fit him, so I sang: 'Oh! Suzanna Oh! Don't you cry for me, for I'm goin' to Louisiana my 2x4 see!!' Now I realize one must know what a 2x4 is before you get the full impact of my song. A 2x4 is simply a piece of wood 2"thick x 4" long… Just like my Uncle Ed used many, many times to build his houses and buildings!! By the way, the real words to the song I sang were right except for the 2x4. The song actually says 'I'm goin' to Louisiana *my* *true love for to see!'* It's quite understandable to make the mistake I did while living and breathing 2x4's with Uncle Ed.

Speaking of 2x4'a and Uncle Ed, I want you to meet him the best way I can, through the stories I tell. He was probably 5'10" tall, robust and weighed a bit over 200 pounds. Evidently he inherited his father's (my grandpa Dalton) eyes, for they were the same loving blue, I remember my grandfather having. Uncle Ed's formal education was completed in the eighth grade. From then on, he became a self-made man, and carpentry must have helped him throughout years. He moved from Kentucky in 1924 to start his new life in Clearwater, Florida and built the house at 721 New York Street where I lived with him and Aunt Beulah. He and Aunt Beulah lived in that same house for all of his years.

When I came to be a part of the family, I was not there as a guest. No! I had to carry some weight, and Uncle Ed knew how to dole it out without making me feel put-upon. That came not only for the respect I had for this sweet, sweet man, but he had a weapon, a thick yard stick with raised numbers on it that he applied freely to my behind when I went astray. It didn't happen very often, but often enough that I remember it well. The last time I remember him applying the yard stick to my back side came one night when I missed my 10 o'clock pm curfew. He had to get up the next morning and needed his sleep which he could not get until I came home and he heard the front door close. Yeah, I remember that time...I could read the numbers from that infamous yard stick on my behind. I checked it out in the full length mirror in our bathroom before I went to bed. I could actually read the numbers on my behind!!! That's not easy punishment to forget.

If Uncle Ed wanted his work shop straightened, he called on me; when he had a bunch of wood to stack, or restack, he called on me. Other duties included helping Aunt Beulah in the kitchen. Helping do the dishes was one chore, but I also learned how to cook really good food. Aunt Beulah was a pro. Then I advanced to making cornbread every night from scratch. This was Uncle Ed's favorite. He often used it as dessert by crumbling it into a glass of milk. Out of doors could be pure torture in Clearwater in the summertime, but that didn't mean I could neglect to mow the yard and weed the flower beds. One thing I learned very early on was that I must wear shoes when mowing, or actually even walking in the yard. There is this pesky little sticker called a sand spur, and they hurt. Since we had never even heard of air conditioning, the only way to cool down was to step in the shower… but not for long, because we needed to preserve our water supply, or wait until evening, after supper when we would all go to the beach for a nice cool dip in the Gulf of Mexico.

Uncle Ed wore bathing trunks and an undershirt when he went swimming, and one evening when we were there taking our refreshing dip, Uncle Ed said he felt something jump up on his chest. Then he started moving around, wanting to be rid of whatever it was that was attacking him. It turned out to be one of his best fishing days, because it was mullet that jumped on his chest and two or three of them even got inside his undershirt. We all had a good laugh from that one! But Uncle Ed was serious when it came to having me do pretty tough chores, while teaching me all about responsibility. But I think the worse job I had to help him with was when he decided the house needed a new roof…Yes, indeed, I was up on the housetop with him every day, no matter how hot, until WE had a new roof on our house. Those were often difficult chores and only made worse by the intense heat of the Florida sun, but I am thankful for the lessons I was taught.

In the winter time when I wasn't stacking wood or sorting nails or performing all the other chores on our 'to-do' list, Aunt Beulah took the time to teach me how to crochet, sew, iron my own clothes and even knit.

Uncle Ed was never a wealthy man, moneywise, but he had a heart of gold to go with those beautiful blue eyes, that would make me literally sick to my stomach if I ever thought of hurting him in anyway. I remember that he told me one time that his take-home pay was $85.00 a week, as he worked as a subcontractor for Robert M. Thompson, one of the big contractors who in large part put the buildings in down-town Clearwater, Florida, also on Clearwater Beach such as the still functioning, Coronado Hotel as well as many other businesses and residential homes.

With that $85.00 pay, first came out tithing to the church, then

Aunt Beulah was given $20 to figure out how to feed our family for the week, even if we had expected or unexpected guests. My cut was 50 cents a week. This paid for my lunch at school at 10 cents a day!! Money was supplied for any school supplies I needed. And Uncle Ed took care of the rest of his money and we really had a good life; always plenty to eat and to wear, a nice house and even up to date car. Thinking back, it is difficult to think of the inevitable struggles to make ends meet. But, again I learned so much in my years with Uncle Ed and Aunt Beulah, and I am so grateful for my time with them.

Uncle Ed always liked to mess *with* things and 'tinker' as he would call it. He always wanted to be on the cutting edge of whatever new thing was going, and at this time, it was the ability to cut a record. He got his recording machine whereby he could put a blank 'plastic' (?) disc on his turn table and then he lowered the needle and it would cut the sounds into the disc. After he cut the sounds into the disc, he could somehow play back what he had recorded. It was quite the thing at that time and Uncle Ed was like a kid with a new toy. He recorded the music sessions, but he didn't stop there. We all loved to sing old gospel songs and one of our favorites was "Life Is like a Mountain Railroad" and since we lived between the Atlantic Coast Line railroad to our East and the Seaboard railroad to our West, we had access to train sounds. Whistles and all! And Uncle Ed recorded some of those sounds, then had Joys sing the song and Uncle Ed felt like he had just about hit the top in recording artists! Oh, yeah, we did have fun! We even recorded a song or two where Joys and I harmonized and then wonder of wonders, he recorded Joys harmonizing with herself.

One night while the group was practicing at our house...another incident where Bobbie set me up and *I* barely avoided getting in trouble. We often drew a crowd from the neighborhood at the music sessions, so there were several kids around. It was an evening in October, close to Halloween, and Bobbie had the bright idea that she would put a sheet over herself and stand on our back porch, then send a message for me to come around the house to the back porch, which I did, and there she was in her sheet and scared the living jeebies out of me...and I yelled! Guess what...the constable, ever ready to defend the public, jumps, as best he could, and ran to the back porch with his pistol drawn. I have always felt that Bobbie should really have gotten her britches paddled, but, no, not sweet little Bobbie! I almost got in trouble for screaming! How's that for proper punishment?

With Joys' help, I too, learned to play the piano. I even took lessons for a bit, but I did not have the patients to do it like it should be done. I wanted to play like my teacher after only a few weeks' lessons. Of course she took the time to study for a while in Germany! Later, I decided I would take the time to teach myself all I could, and it resulted in my ability to play well enough that I played for our church, Sunday school, Vacation Bible School and most of the time just for my own entertainment. I still have my piano and love to play even though it is a struggle what with arthritis and general lack of practice. But I do love it and hope that my grandkids and great grand kids will take an interest in piano. You will never be lonely if you do. Music has been in my family from as far back as I can remember. Anytime my mother's family got together, somebody sat at the piano and everybody else picked up a book and sang and sang and sang!! Later I will tell you how music played a part in my relationship with Gail who would later become my husband...that will come after a while.

One more bit about our patriotic efforts in WWII. Our country was very united and most every able bodied male 18 years to 36 years old went into some branch of the service to do whatever they could. Pete, Arnie's dad, was probably one of the oldest members, as he was 36 when he went in. In his everyday life he was a carpenter, so he went into the Sea Bees. This was a unit of the military that went places before the troops got there and built housing for them. Interestingly, Pete was born and raised in Florida where the weather is almost always comfortable, and when he entered the service, he took his basic training in Providence, Rhode Island. That is a state in the upper north east and on the Atlantic Ocean so it gets pretty cold. Then after his basic training, he was sent to the Aleutian Islands, just off the coast of Alaska, an even colder place. Needless to say, Pete was glad when the war was over and he could come back to his warm home in Florida.

Being patriotic took several forms. One was that most people had their own garden. We called them Victory Gardens. Everybody was doing the best they could to keep things running smoothly at home while all the men were away. We had a victory garden at our school. The Future Farmers class was loaned some property to garden. The boys planted vegetables and then different classes would go from time to time and pick the vegetables and then the classes would meet in the big room (our auditorium) and we would shell the peas, snap the beans and whatever else we could do to prepare these vegetables and sing patriotic songs before the veggies were ready to go downstairs to the kitchen where the mothers of the school kids would can these vegetables for us kids to eat. It really was a great effort and a lot of fun and really good fresh food, and a nice well-cooked, delicious lunch only cost 10 cents. It would be nice if we could go back to doing some of the things like this again. Don't you think this would make us all enjoy school lunches more knowing that we had raised the food and the moms had prepared it instead of some regimented program from the government?

Being close to the military bases and since Clearwater was on the Gulf of Mexico, we had to do things that people who lived in the Midwest, where I live today, didn't need to do. One was that we would have mock air raids from time to time. When the sirens sounded, we had to turn out all the lights in the house that we could. But we also had thick dark window blinds, so that if lights had to be on, it wouldn't shine so much. Also in case you were out driving at night during a raid, all the vehicles had to cover as much of their head lights on their cars as they could and still be able to see to drive. Again, Uncle Ed, wanting to be unique, designed and eagle for the covering on his car head lights.

Sometimes it was just the sirens, but other times planes would fly over our houses and drop sacks of something harmless, so we could get a feel of what it might be like if the enemy, in this case Hitler, from Germany, got close enough to bomb us. Patriotism even went as far as the clothes we wore. Everybody wanted to wear as much Red, White and Blue as they could, to show their patriotism...Bobbie, Mary Helen and I all three had Red, White and Blue dresses that out mamma's made. It was interesting that we all three had the colors, but each dress style was different and one dress had mainly red, while the other had mainly blue and the other mainly white...and this was not planned by the mamma's, it just turned out that way. Bobbie, Mary Helen and I always wore our patriotic dresses on the same day. Often that day was Monday, because every Monday morning shortly after the school bell rang. The classes marched outside the building to the flag pole, where usually either boy scouts or girl scouts would raise the flag. We would say our pledge of allegiance to our beautiful flag and sing the National Anthem ...The Star Spangled Banner. Oh, how I wish our schools did this again!

What a great way to start our week. And in addition, <u>each morning</u> in our class room we had someone read a passage from the Bible, we would say the Lord's Prayer and then have our flag salute....***everyday***, and no one objected. And we didn't have crime in our school, and we also had the Ten Commandments posted in the hallway walls. Oh, my we are missing out today! I am so glad to not only have been a part of this, but to also be able to tell you how it really was, because, I understand that a lot of the things that you are being taught in school today just aren't the true story! And some absurd law had The Ten Commandments removed from *ALL* eyes! And we couldn't pray in school anymore. And anyone with two eyes can see the turning of our culture since these elements, which were so vital to the standards of morality, were taken from us. I never could understand what was so offensive about having a set of, not suggestions, but COMMANDMENTS from our Creator God hanging in plain view to remind us how we should act out our daily lives. What a sad and unnecessary loss!! Was that nonsense really made a law by our *SUPREME COURT system??*

These were just some of the interesting things that I could remember about life during WWII, when the country was united and everyone took care of his neighbor. Many families were broken up due to deaths during the war, but my family was very fortunate. Many of the men who had seen some of the real battles and bombings came home without major injuries. My brother Harvel had gotten a disease from having to sleep in the trenches in New Guinea that many times held water and caused what was known as 'jungle rot'. Not a very glamorous name, but this was not a very glamorous war. This disease causes him a lot of itching and peeling of the skin and a lot of discomfort especially on his hands and feet, but he was able to keep it pretty well controlled with medication.

One other problem that could have been worse than it was, was that there was a lot of time when the men were stuck someplace with nothing to do, so they started drinking quite a bit and with many it carried over into their civilian life and some had to have treatment to keep it from becoming a bigger problem. But overall, we were blessed! They all came home alive and without arms or legs missing, as was the case with far too many. Then there were those who gave their lives on a battle field in a part of the world they had never seen before, again, we were blessed.

War was over and that year, 1945, at Christmas time, I had the happiest time of my life. I had gotten a phone call from my younger brother, Eutra, and he was coming to Florida to see me! I had not seen him for over three years! And Harvle would also be there with me for that Christmas. I remember the day Harvle came home from the service. He got to Clearwater somehow and took a bus that brought him to New York Street where I lived. I remember so well seeing him come up the street in his military uniform and a suitcase in his hand. I nearly tore the screen door down as I ran out to meet him!! By Christmas he was already living in Clearwater since his discharge, and was working a trade in a leather goods shop. And when I got the phone call from Eutra, I wanted to just run around the neighborhood and cry for joy and tell everybody that my brother would be home soon. I actually pretty much did just that. The only place I knew to run was up the street where my cousins, the Walkers lived. I remember that about half way up there I was so overcome with joy that I stopped in the middle of the road and just stood there and cried...and cried...for joy...my brother was coming to see me!!!

After that, life seemed to just go along. Bobbie and I still had fights, and I was in the Girl Scouts and just had a pretty normal life. We did not have sidewalks on New York Street and, remember how I said that I loved to roller skate? Well, there was a very upper class neighborhood a couple of miles from our house called Bellaire Estates, where several wealthy people and some movie stars lived...and they had sidewalks. So we, usually Mary Helen, Bobbie and I, would ride our bikes to Bellaire Estates, and skate all over their beautiful sidewalks. I never did see any of the movie stars. I don't think they were there very often, but Lana Turner was one who lived there, and Fernando Llamas was another and some others I have forgotten their names and you probably never heard of them either, but we enjoyed their sidewalks and no one ever complained.

Also in that neighborhood which was right on the bay side of the Gulf of Mexico, there were some interesting streams, and coves and some small caves coming out from the bay. Now, we never told our folks about our secret places because we figured they thought they would be too dangerous...which they probably were...and as with the incident of the 'rub-a-dub-dub, three girls in the tub' event, we managed to get into some trouble.

I guess it really was scary, we just didn't think so, but on one of our ventures, I slid down a bank and into a little stream and it scared the daylights out of others. But they managed to pull me out and, the of course, there was nothing to do, but go home and face the music. My clothes were muddy and I had some scrapes and scratches, but nothing serious, but I did get punished and so did the others...we were forbidden to EVER go back to that place again. Actually, if anything serious had happened, there was no way anybody knew where we were. There were no cell phones back then. So by all rights, our punishment was just, because our folks were scared, too! But we still were allowed to go over and roller-skate. It was also fun just to ride our bikes around the beautiful homes.

Also in that same area was a hotel that is still there today. I don't know if it still has the same claim to fame as then, but it was at that time the largest wooden hotel around. Don't remember if it was just in our area, or in the state of Florida, or even the nation or the world, but it was big and beautiful...The Belleview Biltmore Hotel! Actually, years later, Sarah, Elana and I went to this hotel and sat on one of the big porches and had a glass of tea...much like dining with the rich...we felt quite fashionable, and elegant!

With all the excitement, fun and even the serious times I mentioned...

we also had to contend with hurricanes, at least once a year. There have been hurricanes of tremendous destruction; however, it seemed we were spared the bad stuff. We got out of school and wasted no time running around it the yard dancing amongst the flying pine needles as they blew from the tall pine trees. But **watch out!** Once in a while you just might get bonked with a pine cone or two. But to we young ones, it was fun. Often at night the storms worsened, and since my cousins lived just up the street from us, we all got together and played games as we listened to the weather forecast on the radio. The games were usually played with the women and children, since the able bodied men would be out in the neighborhood boarding up windows and tying down trees. It seemed we were always able to make a fun time even in the midst of the bad.

In the summertime our family would go back to visit relatives in Scottsville, and one of the highlights for me was getting to go to school with Aunt Beulah's niece and nephew, Dorcas and Wayne.Lyles. We were close to the same age, and since they were from farm families, their school started in July and went until February. Another interesting fact is that they went to a ONE ROOM SCHOOL! You probably remember seeing these on Little House on the Prairie. On the TV series the school name was Walnut Grove. The name of the one room school I visited was Briarfield. Well it was great because I had the opportunity to go to school with them. The younger children were in the front of the room and the older ones went progressively to the back, all the way to the 6th grade level.

There were about 15 or 16 kids in the entire class room, and one teacher. There were several of these one-room schools throughout the area close to the farms. The day always started with Bible reading, prayer and flag salute, like I had been accustomed to in Florida. Then the teacher would give the different levels something to work on as she worked first with the youngest ones.

There was no running water, nor indoor toilet, so to go to the bathroom we had to go to a little building out behind the school house. As for drinking water, we had to go a spring of water where we could get a bucket full and bring it back for the class to have. There were no individual cups or glasses, we had a long handled aluminum dipper...all used the same one to drink from, and I don't remember anyone getting sick from it.

Since I was a visitor, I was allowed to go with whoever went to the spring to get the water. It was usually a pretty long walk through the woods, but the water was always clean, clear and cold! Usually it was one of the boys who went to carry the bucket, but a couple of others went along in case there was any trouble. It was just nice to get to walk through the woods and fields.

The school had a softball team and they played against other one-room schools in the area. When we went from our school to another we usually took a wagon and somebody's horse pulled us there. Sometimes some farmers would take us in their pick-up truck. It was great fun. And again, since I was a visitor, I was allowed to play ball, too. Not only that, I was a pretty good ball player and I remember one of the teams one time made a remark about my being there gave our school an unfair advantage, but for the most part, everybody got along just great and we had fun. That was the main thing! The little school was very picturesque, and very much a part of our past lives.

This particular time of visiting the one room school was after I moved to Florida, and before that, when I still lived in Scottsville, we lived in town and had a regular school, much like the ones we have now, a red brick building a couple of stories high. So it was really a special time for me to actually be a part of the one-room school atmosphere. Sometimes I think we would be better off if things were more like they were back then...but I am glad that I had the experience and can tell you about it...hopefully, it will make it more real for you!

Visiting with the Lyle family was fun, too. That is where I learned to like buttermilk. Even though the lady of the house was not my real aunt, I still called her Aunt Lucy. Her husband was Uncle Frank. Aunt Lucy churned milk like Aunt Nora did...remember; I talked about her a while back. But Aunt Lucy made buttermilk. It was called buttermilk mainly because it had actual bits of butter in it, but also with buttermilk, it was a little sour. That is why they called the regular milk 'sweet milk'. Either way, when the milk came from the cows on the farm, it was the best EVER!! The chips of butter in the buttermilk were left, on purpose of course, but most of the butter bits were strained out of the milk before they made the buttermilk and then it was placed into butter mold and was soon ready for some homemade bread or biscuits. That had to be the best tasting butter you could imagine. It makes me hungry just to write about it...YUM, YUM!! Oh, my goodness...I want a bite of that NOW!!! And as good as it tasted, it also made the whole house smell wonderful!! You know what!!!! I think I just might make some homemade bread and maybe I can find somebody who still knows how to make the butter...Want some????

I guess I had better move on or I will just take a nap here at my desk, dreaming about hot homemade bread and delicious home churned butter!!

Let's see...where on earth can I go to get my mind out of the kitchen before my body decides to follow??

Maybe before we go back to Florida, I will take you back to Aunt Pearl and Uncle Ira's farm...with their 10 kids. Aunt Pearl was related to me through my father's side of the family...the Barger's, and she was a twin to Uncle Earl. There was always something to do and plenty of room to do it in...if nothing else but wander around the farm. Cousin Billy D. was a twin to sister, Jenny B., and one day when he was milking a cow, he asked me if I wanted some really fresh milk. So he turned one of the cow's teats toward me and squeezed and I had my mouth open to receive the freshest milk you could possibly get. That was neat.

Mealtime at their house was an adventure also. In the kitchen along with a big wood stove where Aunt Pearl did all the cooking, there was a big cabinet that held whatever cooking utensils she needed and another cabinet with dishes and silverware. But the grandest thing of all was the table that was big enough for EVERYBODY to sit down and eat, and it seemed that no matter how many were there, there was always room for them! Isn't that the way God works in Christian homes? This reminds me of something that happened at our house in Dale one Sunday. I had fixed a pot roast with the usual potatoes and carrots and I don't remember what else, but we already had several for dinner and just as we were soon to be sitting for dinner, we had company. It was a couple we knew well who had come to Dale to visit the husband's mother who was in the nursing home. Their daughter and son-in-law were with them and of course, I asked them to stay for dinner. They didn't want to intrude on us, but easily accepted the invitation. I looked at what I had prepared and wondered if there could possibly be enough, but told our new guests all I needed to do was add some more potatoes and carrots…I couldn't make the meat grow and that was what I was concerned about. Time came to eat and we had our dining table filled and even set up a special table in the living room. Now, I did not sit there and watch the pot roast grow, but I tell you the honest truth. From one platter of dinner we fed 10 people when I had planned for 6 and had left overs! God does things like that, doesn't He?

But backing up many years to my telling you about mealtime at Uncle Ira's and Aunt Pearl's, we didn't have TV to divert our attention from our food. We all sat around the table, Uncle Ira usually said the prayer and then some of the most delicious food ever was passed around and everybody had plenty to eat. If it was evening time, our time at the table was spent talking about all the things that had happened to us during the day. Some had some funny stories, some had some unpleasant experiences, but the main thing was that we all talked and we all also listened and were genuinely concerned about each other.

When dinner was over, the dogs got to eat the scraps…and there usually were some, and then the dirty dishes did NOT go into a dishwasher. No. There was a table with a big pan full of hot soapy water and another big pan full of hot clean water. Someone washed, someone rinsed others dried and put away. The water did not come from a faucet either. No, it was heated in a big kettle on the stove, taken from a pump that was also in the kitchen. When supper was over and the dishes put away, it was time to just sit back and relax until time to go to bed.

Now with 10 kids, there were several kids sleeping in the same bed, but my favorite spot was on a pallet on the floor right in front of the front screened door, so I could see outside and watch lightening bugs and whatever else I could find in the dark. Believe me, if the moon wasn't shining, it was really dark. They did not have any street lights, and they didn't even have any outside lights…so it could be really dark, you could hardly see your hand in front of your face, and that is when somebody would decide to tell ghost stories. And so the night went... then the next morning was a breakfast to never be forgotten. Fresh ham and sausage, or sometimes country ham, homemade biscuits, gravy, GRITS and eggs...now these were fresh eggs. Uncle Ira would go out to the hen house and come in with eggs in his pockets and some even in the bib of his overalls. It took a lot of ham & eggs and biscuits to feed that crew, but boy was it good. I remember going back to Uncle Ira and Aunt Pearls, many years later. They had arranged for any of the 10 kids to come and bring food. There was food galore!! So much food that in the summertime, it was served from a flatbed trailer that some- one backed into the yard and someone else hauled in enough chairs one would have thought it was a community gathering, when it was only *family!*

Uncle Ira only had one arm. He got it caught in a wheat thrasher, or something. This happened a time before I ever knew him, because the first memories I have of him was that he, being my loving uncle, wanted to give me a hug when we got together, and I was only 4 or 5 years old and remember being a little afraid of ...not him, but he had a leather extension on the stub...that is what bothered me. But over the years I got used to it and it never bothered me at all. Later on he didn't wear anything over the stub, and even that didn't bother me. I was always just amazed at all he could do with only one arm, and it was his right arm. It certainly didn't keep him from gathering eggs for the hungry crew. I'm sure he was glad to have enough boys to do the work he could no longer do....what a family!

Oh, my! I just remembered a funny, funny story about the 'telephone'. This happened to a friend of mine. Remember, even at the time of this story, we are living in an era when telephones in the house were minimal...usually one per household, as was the case here. Well, women especially should know that *every* telephone call is important! We did not have the aggravating ROBO calls like today, so this was an important call...important enough that this sweet lady friend felt compelled to step out of her bath tub (soapy body etal) and get to that phone before it quit ringing. Only thing is, on her way down the hall (wrapped only in a bath towel), the poor lady slipped on her soapy feet and slid about half a mile down the hall, and ended up missing her call and even suffered a few bruises...I did exaggerate about the distance down the hall...according to the lady herself...it just felt like it! Danged old inventions!!!

Now I guess I need to get back to Clearwater, Florida, because I loved living there, and even learned to love going to school, in spite of my cousin Bobbie.

My family belonged to the church of the Nazarene and I soon became a part of a group of young people that I cherished the rest of my life. There were 8 or 10 of us and we hung together sort of like a family, like I guess we really were. But then came the time when we girls decided that the boys might make nice boyfriends. It was funny how we just sort of wandered into a teenage relationship without any guidance. It just happened and no fights. Our group grew from time to time, because living in Florida, a lot of people wanted to come down there from various places up north in the winter time. Some went back in the spring while others became permanent residents, making our group even larger and more fun.

The Nazarene church was pretty strict on what we were allowed to do and not to do. Much of which most of us could never understand what harm there was in bowling, or even roller skating!! Oh, my, you should have heard the warnings we got when a temporary roller rink sat up in town and not too far from our church!! But the church's position was that most bowling alleys were in with bars, and the church was adamant against any form of liquor.

And in roller skating there was music and we were moving our bodies in rhythm to the music.

The sad thing about restrictions such as the church held is that people, not unlike Adam and Eve, want to taste the forbidden fruit, and many within the church did a lot of things the church was against. But honestly, our group of teenagers held to the restrictions and still had great fun. A few of our group even got married, but most ventured out into other parts of the world and found mates there, as I did. When you think about it, God has a plan for us and he has a mate for us, and he brought me together with mine in a most unusual way...one that only God could instigate! Do you want to hear that story? Well...Once upon a time...

Yes, I had a boyfriend in Clearwater, too. His name was Jo Ed Messer, and he was the preacher's son! Actually there was a bit of difference in our ages...about 6 years...and at my age then, that was a lot of difference, sadly, Joe found a beautiful girl who was closer to his age and they got married. Now, I was only 16 years old, but love...I mean your first *real* love, can hit you pretty hard, and mine was no exception. I really felt I was in love with Jo, and even with the age difference, Jo really loved me. It was just the wrong time, and Jo wasn't the one God had in mind for me to marry. God knew exactly what I needed in a husband.

Now at age 16 it just might seem strange for me to be talking about finding a husband. There are several reasons. One, at that point in history, it was not unusual for a girl to marry at age 16 or 17. I had no real profession that drew me to wanting to go to school and get training, and besides, I didn't have the money and, although I think Uncle Ed would have done what he could to help me get an education, it would have been a hardship on him, too. Not only that, I had been encouraged...well maybe not encouraged, but at least I was told many times by Aunt Beulah that since she was only 15 when she got married, she didn't feel she could hold me back from marriage any time after I turned 15. That is probably why losing my first love was so hard. But God knew what He was doing all along...as He always does, and He gave us the perfect opportunity to change things and even places, which would definitely help me ease away from having to accept the fact that Jo had married someone else!

Remember my two brothers, Harvle and Eutra? These two boys were older than me and I had always looked up to them, especially without my father who had been killed when I was only 6 weeks old. So having grown up with only substitute father relationships these guys were my solid rock. Harvle had not married yet and he was 27 years old and lived in St. Petersburg, Fl., just a short way from Clearwater, but Eutra, who was 8 years older than me, was married, had a small daughter and was living in Indianapolis, IN. Some heads got together and decided it would be good if Harvle and I moved to Indianapolis and lived with or close to Eutra and his family. After all, we had lost all of the rest of our family and it only seemed like a good thing to do for us to be closer together. So Harvle and I packed our bags and moved to Indianapolis.

While we were still in the process of getting our 'family' settled there, a cousin of mine, Buell, who at that time was living in Dale, IN, and was the pastor of the Methodist Church in Dale, came to visit us in Indy. He asked me if I might consider coming to Dale with him and living with their family because he had 2 children, ages 6 and 10, and they could use the help. Well, what is there to think about?? I am so used to picking up and moving some place, why not go for it? Besides, this visit was over Christmas break at school. No, I didn't get out of attending school just because I moved. I started my senior year in high school at Emmerick Manual Training High School in Indianapolis, and when I tell you how I got to school, you will know why it didn't take me long to decide to move again. Also, Buell had said that since this was break time at school, if I didn't like living in Dale, he would bring me back to Indy. We were not too concerned about Harvle, after all, he was 27 years old, had served in the army during World War II and had been living on his own in St Pete...yeah, he would be OK, so why not give it a try?

A short time back I said I would tell you how I got to school in Indy. It is my hope that none of you kids ever have to get to school the way I did....No, it wasn't walking 2 miles up hill both ways in 6" of snow... actually that would have been fun compared to the way I went. First, the world was a bit safer back then, but it was still dangerous in a big city, and believe me, Indy was the biggest city I had ever been to. Every school morning I would get up about 6am and get myself ready and walk about ½ mile to catch a city bus to downtown, where from there I would walk possibly 8 or 10 blocks, while it was still pretty dark, and had to go through a couple of tunnels, making it even more scary. I did not like it!!! But I survived!

Fortunately, as in many cases in my life, someone came to my rescue and I moved to Dale to live with Buell and his family for whatever period of time the Lord had designed for me. The family life was good, and yes I had to go back to school. After all, this was my senior year...at last I would be free from school!! But I say that rather jokingly, because I really did like school, and at Dale, the senior class had about 40+ students, and I fit right in with all the functions. I got one of the lead parts in the senior play and, at the request of my Government teacher. I entered an oratorical contest, my topic being "Our Framing Fathers". I still have a copy of the speech someplace in my files and I won at the first level, but a guy from another school won first place overall.

I remember riding into Dale and I fell in love with the town instantly. It seemed so idyllic, like something you would see in the movies. Even though I had been born in a small town, it still was quite different from Dale. It gave me a feeling I have difficulty expressing, other than falling in love with this little laid back community. Yes! I wanted to become a part of this. I knew right away that I was not going back to Indianapolis and hopefully not ever any big city. I was born a small town girl and I liked it very much, thank you! And I wanted to become a part of the workings of this little place in any way I could...and I did! This included things such as becoming the wife of the most eligible bachelor in town, giving life to three great children and becoming as much a part of whatever they were in as I could, such as PTA and Band Booster president, organizing the sock hop so the kids could dance on what was well known as the 'sacred hardwood floor' where the life breath of Dale seemed to be on Friday nights in the winter time. This was known as Hoosier basketball. If you were not a basketball fan, surely you were not a Hoosier!

Quite often I would fry up a batch of chicken and head out with the kids, be it music contest or swim meet. Often I would team up with my friend, Norma Ficker and we would get our big roll of paper and spread it out on the cafeteria tables and create some sort of signs that would boost whatever effort was tops at the time...and had lots of fun doing it! And the kids appreciated our efforts.

There was a special process I went through to acquire the rights to the sock hop on Friday nights after the ball game…football or basketball. As a matter of fact our very first sock hop came on the night we crowned Barb Guth football queen. We played North Posey (I believe) and I also believe we won. The visiting team had been invited to participate in the dance and many stayed. The school bus waited for them and we were at the beginning of something the kids enjoyed for several years. But back to the process…I contacted Ron Etienne, who was a teacher at Dale High School and also Student Counselor. He gathered the members of the council and we met in one of the school rooms and laid out some guidelines we felt would hold us all accountable, yet give the kids some rules they knew were necessary to follow or not be allowed at the dance. Each student signed in and if they left before the dance was over, they had to sign out so if anything happened to them they would have something to show when they left the premises. This was also a time before blue jeans and slacks were accepted wear. So another of the rules was that the girls could wear dress slacks, and the guys dress pants…no jeans!

The rules also required that at least two sets of parents should attend the dance as chaperones. Boy! Were we tough!! The dances were a hit for several years, but as most things, we move on to something else.

Another of the local functions that appealed to me was the choral club. Music had always played an important part in my life. Early on, I sang in church choirs, then advanced to solos, and even had a trio with two of my friends. We were really pretty good…good enough to sing on the local radio station several times and even entertain at Chamber of Commerce meetings on Clearwater Beach. Also in my musical 'career', I sang at weddings and funerals, and in the bath tub, and in the rain, and just about any place the moment hit me! So when I found that Dale had a choral club I joined, along with my cousin Bernice, the pastor's wife.

Now things happen in strange ways to me but this is one for the books! One night at Choral Club rehearsal I realized I had left my music book at home. There was a nice looking young man named Gail Witte, who sang with the group and I was bold enough to ask him if he would drive me to my house to pick up my music. He did...and after practice, a group of singers filled his car and we went to a restaurant in Huntingburg for some refreshments. Now this nice looking young man had a girlfriend that I was not aware of, and since he had been so nice as to take me to get my music, I thought it might be nice to sit by him in the front seat of his car. His girlfriend had other ideas...she beat me to the car...but not to be deterred, I immediately hopped in the back seat, behind him...I knew what she was doing!!! He drove us to a place in Huntingburg, about 8 miles up the road, called the Palace of Sweets. This was a really neat place with décor reminiscent of several years back with the juke box and ice cream parlor type tables and chairs. And a fine time was had by all, although there might have been a little bit of tension in the air.

The very next Sunday, I was 'babysitting' my 6 year old cousin and a friend and I went walking and I asked her to show me where Gail Witte lived. We walked by his house. It was one of the nicest houses in town and big, too. My friend Louise, my cousin Mary Ellen, and I walked over to the city park on our way home, and who should be at the park but Gail Witte. Of course we stopped to speak and he asked if we would like to go to the restaurant for a cup of coffee. Well, the restaurant was closed so, realizing I was new in town, this nice young man suggested that he take us to the Lincoln Boyhood National Memorial, In Lincoln City, IN. I had long heard of Abraham Lincoln and was interested in history and government so this was quite an educational event for me. It was educational in more ways than one. On our way walking back to the car, after having toured Nancy Hanks' (Abraham Lincoln's mother) grave and other places around the park, Gail asked if I would like to go to a movie with him that evening...umh...'sure, I would love to!' I didn't bother to ask about what his 'girlfriend' might think...I'm smarter than that!!

Yes, we went to a movie, but I can't remember the name of it, I was just enjoying the fact that I had won the favor of this nice young eligible bachelor, even if only momentarily. He had me home on time and told me he was leaving the next morning, driving a semi-truck to Alabama, where he and another driver from the mill, Sonny, would take grain to

Kentucky and haul back some lumber, and his next words were, 'I'll be back Thursday afternoon, and would you like to go out for dinner with me?' ...umh...'sure, I'd love to!' Wow! How lucky can one girl get? I was dancing all week and waiting impatiently for Thursday, March 4, 1950, to come, and believe it or not, it finally got there! It just seemed like an awfully long several days!!

Again, I don't remember what restaurant we went to, but I think it was in Evansville. Remember, I am still pretty new to the area. He drove me over the bridge of the Ohio River to Henderson, KY...just sort of sight-seeing. On the way home we parked in a small, well lighted parking area and just sat and talked for a while, when all of a sudden, he turned to me and said..."Jean, will you marry me??" OOOOOHHHBOY!!! Now what do I do? Well, I did what any red-blooded American girl who just might be ready for marriage would do...I said "Yes, I would be honored!" WOW! And double WOW! No...I actually said..."What took you so long?" What an evening! Little did he know that I had fallen in love with him on first sight! We were together as much as possible from then on. He wanted to let the world know that we were engaged to be married, but I was only 17 and still in high school, and legally under age, so he told me he would give me the engagement ring right after graduation. Well, that started another loooonnnnggg period of waiting!, but it was worth it. Let me take a bit of time here to tell you more about the man I was going to marry: He was 6'1" tall, dark hair, with a nice wave. He had a winning smile, almost as though he had something else to say, but, for some reason didn't. He was sort of a mystery man and intriguing!!

The result of that "Love-at-first-sight" event:

*Married by cousin Rev. Buell Dalton in the Methodist
church, Dale Indiana, August 6th 1950*

I had been told that on Monday's I would see him at the back door of the Mill where he was reading from the orders he had taken from customers throughout the area, and had the employees loading a truck so these products, flour, corn meal, horse, hog and chicken feed, could be delivered to their recipients the next day. One more thing I was told that I could recognize him by was that he whistled while he worked!! As I had walked by the Mill going home from school, I saw this and liked it very much!! In learning more about him and it seemed the more I learned, the more I liked what I was getting. I learned that he had served his time in the service of our country at Terre Haute, Indiana College. He was in the Naval Air Corp, but was fortunate enough to not have to go into the battle of WWII. Having finished school at Terre Haute, he earned a bachelor's degree from the University of Illinois at Champaign, IL. After graduating from UI, he returned to Dale to go into the milling business with his dad. His dad, Jake Witte, had bought the building and a nice sized lot on a prime corner of the town of Dale, IN. in 1930, for $5,ooo.00. I was beginning to feel like God was smiling on me to bring me to this little town in Indiana and hand me the town's most eligible bachelor.

Little did either of us realize how expensive I would become throughout our marriage, especially medically. He was introduced to his first taste of it in May, 1950, just after we became officially engaged. Since moving from the beautiful weather in Florida and encountering the unpredictable Indiana weather, I often had problems with a sore throat. Finally it got so bad I had to see the one doctor in the town of Dale, who just happened to be a friend of my soon-to-be new family. After Dr. Barrow took one look at my throat, he insisted I have my tonsils removed...but I had no money to pay for the doctor, surgery, hospital stay, etc. But Gail said to me that since I was almost his, I should not worry about the medical bills. So we chose a day for the removal of my tonsils and, surprising to me, the doctor, after driving me to the hospital in his nice big Lincoln, took me in the back door of the hospital, into a small room and gave me a hospital gown to put on. There were no nurses around...just the doctor and me! Since I had never worn one of these gowns, I had no idea which way they were to open, so I put it on and tied it in the front, with much of me exposed. The doctor laughed and told me I should tie it in the back. Then Dr. Barrow told me to just sit in the chair...the only one in this small room, and the surgery would be over with very soon. At this point, he brought out a giant needle and told me to 'open wide'!! Surprisingly it was not very painful. This was the numbing medicine. When the numbing medicine had taken effect, he gave me a little pan to hold by my mouth in case I needed it. As I said before, this was all new to me, so I just followed instructions. Then he again said to *open wide*! Now it was time to close my eyes because he was going to *cut my tonsils out* while I sat on this cold metal chair, and with the gown opening in the back, there was very little protection from the chair. I tried to not think about what he was doing and hoped the numbing medicine had done its job. I guess it did, because, I felt very little pain, and didn't get sick. After the removal of the tonsils, he very astutely stitched each side of my mouth with only 2 stitches. Then he put me in a wheel chair and wheeled me to a room where I could lay down in a nice comfortable bed and have nurses look after me and all the other nice things you get when you become a real patient, including the ice cream I had always heard that tonsillectomy patients get!!

I was only supposed to stay until noon that day and Gail was going to come with the doctor so I could be released to go home for some more TLC (tender loving care). However, things didn't quite work out that way. I started hemorrhaging...what a mess!! But Gail and the doctor arrived at my room on time and they both had been advised of my problem. Now, here comes the really good part...Doc says to Gail: "You hold her back and brace her because I am going to have to stitch these tonsils again, and it will be easier for me to just do it than to stick her twice and just hurt more. And I can also have the stitching done before the medicine would take effect anyway." And so he did! I think I should get an award for bravery and Gail should be given one for something, because he not only held me firmly with one hand, but he told me later, he was sure he had left his hand imprint in the bed frame. This was his introduction to the many, many times in the future he would stand by me as I went through some frightening medical times.

The one thing that got me through all of this was my strong faith in the God I serve, and who protects me, even though He has allowed so many physical problems. I firmly believe that these tests only served to strengthen our bond as a couple and the faith both of us had in God. There were times in my medical history that God performed miracles, and I will write about some of these later. But after the tonsillectomy, I went back to my home with Buell and Bernice, I also got my ice cream!

Gail and I had planned to get married in October, which would be right after I turned 18 in September, but his only sister, Fae had accepted a teaching job in Portales, New Mexico and wouldn't be able to be at the wedding in October, so we changed the date to August 6, 1950. Since I was still legally under age I needed the consent of my legal guardian, so I had to write my Uncle Ed in Florida and explain the situation to him and get his consent to get married. It all worked out fantastic. Gail's Aunt Sadie, who was a home Economics Teacher at Dale High School, had by now decided that I was going to be a new addition to the family whether she approved or not. I later thought about the reluctance of Gail's family to embrace me right away. They didn't know anything about me except that I had come to live with the Methodist minister and his wife and that I was a cousin to the minister. That's not much to go on, but Gail and I both knew that we were meant for each other, even though I had to travel around the country to finally find him. What a wonderful man he was!

Aunt Sadie, who was the Home Economics teacher at Dale High School had the perfect initials to fit her profession *SEW,* which stood for *Sarah Ellen Weedman.*

She made my wedding dress, hand covering all thirty something buttons on my wedding gown. She also made the dresses for Mary Ellen who was my flower girl and Fae the maid of honor, and Mary Ann one of Gail's cousins as bridesmaid. Gail's longtime friend, Bill Winkler was best man, and my cousin Buell married us in the Methodist church, right next door to where I had been living these past several months. We drove Gail's dad's 1948 Studebaker on our way to his house for the reception, and then went on our honeymoon trip in his 1949 Plymouth Suburban. We were in style and as happy as two peas in a pod...and, oh yes...as to his *former* girlfriend...she ended up marrying Gail's truck driving buddy, Sonny...and we were all happy!!! Yes, this all worked out great and that is the point I intended to make when I told you about how heartbroken I was when I left Florida and my first love, Jo, behind. But this is how God steps in and gives you something better than you would ever expect. Sadly, Jo died of lung cancer when he was only 34 years old. Had I married him, I would have been all alone, possibly with children. So Gail and I started our lives together on a beautiful sunny Sunday, August 6th, 1950. Believe me God does know best...just listen and watch and see what marvelous things He will do in your life, as He has done in mine.

Gail and I lived in an apartment in Dale, and soon we were waiting for the birth of our first child. I know, because I was sick every morning, every time I saw food, every time I heard certain foods even advertised on the radio. And by the time our baby girl was born, I had lost 18 pounds. And I wasn't very big to begin with! When the time came for us to go to the hospital, Gail couldn't find the key to unlock our apartment door and, frantically ended up having to take the door off its hinges so we could get out. He was much more nervous than I. (I guess he thought I would just drop that little baby before we could even get out of the apartment. He learned a bit different after sitting with me from 8:10am to 5:15 in the afternoon. No. Those little critters just don't drop out...Thank you very much, *EVE!!*

In August 1951 we started to build our house on the property next door to Gail's folks. The property was our wedding gift from his folks. We moved in our house on March 17, 1952...Gail, Jean and #1 daughter, Vikki Lynne, born on July 23, 1951. Two years later we had a little boy that we named Richard Steven, June 30, 1953. Time passed and we were all one happy family, but felt like we needed at least one more little punkin, so on September 21, 1958, Sarah Jean came into our family. Just think how different things would be if we had not decided to extend our family!

There are many things I could tell you about happenings throughout our marriage, I had quite a few medical problems, causing multiple times spent in hospitals around the area and more surgeries that I would like to remember, but God has been exceptionally great to me and I have survived much and am thrilled beyond words to be able to sit here and tell you so much. At this point, I think I will take a break and will get back to more stories soon, so don't leave me, there is more to come!! But first, I have to complete the main purpose of this section of the story, and then I will get back to telling more tales that are true.

Remember I started telling you about falling in love for the first time and how brokenhearted I was when the man I knew I was truly in love with married someone else. Did you follow the sequence of events afterwards? Remember my brother Harvle and I decided to move to Indianapolis to be with our other brother and his wife and daughter, which we did...then my cousin Buell came to visit me in Indy and wanted me to come and live with them...which I did...then how I met a nice young man who was the most eligible bachelor in Dale, and after a very, very short courtship, we were married...well, that solved a big problem in my life, Jo was happily married and living in Florida and no one but God could have caused the sequence of events that brought me to the perfect mate...yes, no one but God Himself could have been so wise and loving to have brought me from what I felt was devastation to a place of love and caring that Gail and I shared from 1950 until the day he died on February 1, 2009...almost 60 years! And we never forgot to give God thanks for bringing us together.

Now, I will get back to telling you some stories that are about funny things that happened in our family and caused us to enjoy life most of the time...it has to do, of course, with your mom's and dad's and aunts and uncles. Get ready...

There was an old saying that 'Children are a joy and a blessing!' They truly are, but sometimes you have to look hard to find the blessing, and it even got to the point that I printed those words out on a piece of paper and stuck them on the bathroom mirror, especially when I was about to pull my hair out over something one child or another had done...but all in all that phrase is true...what would we do without these little 'blessings'?

Still young in our marriage, we were not rich, not with money anyway, and didn't get to buy the things we wanted, and sometimes even things we needed, but simply could not afford. At that time, there were no credit cards, and I believe...no! I *know* that was a blessing. Otherwise, we may have succumbed to the temptation of putting things we felt we just couldn't do without on that little plastic card. Only thing is that once a month you get a notice in the mail that reminds you not only that you spent money you didn't have, but now the question was do we have the money to pay the bill? We did find out later in life that credit cards were a worthwhile thing if you treated them with respect and in accordance with your ability to pay the bill when it came due, remembering also, that if you don't pay the bill, there will be a charge for the money you had actually borrowed from the lending company. So you see, it can become a hassle and sometimes when we get carried away, we want to curse the day the credit card came into being.

Being of the conservative nature that Gail and I both were, we never charged any more on a credit card than we could pay off in full when the payment came due. One thing we did not like was to pay somebody for the privilege of borrowing their money. Now, don't get me wrong. In getting started in life, young couples will almost always find themselves in debt say to the bank, for the money you need to buy your home, or a car. These are things of necessity and we can be thankful for them. There's hardly a couple alive that hasn't had to go in debt at least for their home and/or vehicle. These just have to be purchased wisely, and not out of the bounds of the money you will have coming into your home through your work...in other words, don't go out and buy a Cadillac that might cost $50, 000, when you can have a nice Chevrolet for probably $20,000...or don't buy that beautiful mansion you saw on TV that sells for ONLY $500, 00, when you know you probably couldn't pay that off in your lifetime. Buy one that you can easily make the payments on and let that house grow with you and your family and just watch it become a HOME...one that you will soon own and can enjoy for a long, long time!

Well, I think you get the point of my economics lesson, but I wanted to lay the foundation to let you know that you do not have to have a lot of money to have a great family and plenty of fun.

One experience I remember well was when we had all three of our children, probably ranging in age from about 6 to 11 to 13. It was the coldest night we had seen in years. I think the thermometer was stuck on ZERO...it was cold. And, guess what...our furnace quit working... OH! WHAT WILL WE DO?? Will we freeze to death AND possibly starve? NEVER!!! Here is what we did... Since we were campers, we each had our own sleeping bag. We also had a fireplace in our living room, sooooo, we put on warm clothes sat in front of the fireplace and told stories, and when we got hungry, we got some hot dogs out of the refrigerator and some long forks and had a picnic....LET IT SNOW!

LET IT SNOW! LET IT SNOW!. We were warm, our tummies were full and we were having a great time. We even pretended we were pioneers travelling out through the mountains in the winter and wondering if we would survive! We were also very glad that the furnace man came the next day and fixed our problem. But we knew that if we had another problem, we were sure we could solve it!

Another thing we did for fun that you may have had the chance to do. On a summer night I would pack hot dogs and buns, along with a big container of popcorn and a cooler with drinks and go to the Drive-In Movie! What fun we had, although I imagine the concession stand missed our business. But we were on a limited budget and had to devise ways to have fun that didn't cost much money. Then there were times I would fry some chicken, fix potato salad and bake a cake and we would just drive around southern Indiana until we found a place of interest and had a grand family picnic. Wonderful memories and in the summer the food just tasted better outside.

We had a friend who was a salesman for some product that Gail carried at the Mill. The man's name was Von Kleppinger and he lived in Ohio. Gail invited him over to our house for supper sometimes, even when I wasn't fully prepared for company. I remember the first time he came, we were having beans and cornbread and pork roast. Now that is not a bad meal, but not one I would choose to serve to someone I had only met over in the mill office a time or two…but he came, we ate and everybody enjoyed. And Von, being the nice man that he was, told us to plan to go out to eat the next time he came to town, because he would treat us. What a nice surprise and what a nice man. He at least acted like he really liked our kids and they became pretty fond of him, too. Often when he would come, he would bring a special surprise for the family, like a box of cookies, or candy or something nice. He knew we were still struggling to raise our family and make what money Gail made cover all of our expenses and hopefully have some that we could start saving. He, at this time in his life had reached his pinnacle of success and was a pretty wealthy man. He told us of how it was when he and his wife were first married and didn't have much, so they made time with their kids the center of their entertainment. Simple things like playing games and reading stories and giving baths. Once in a while they could afford a movie...what a treat! But all along they felt that by doing this they would be able to do more later on...and indeed, they did! His most encouraging remark to Gail was that you just keep plugging along and climbing that hill and someday you will reach the top and things will go much better from then on as you coast down!

Von introduced Vikki to her first lobster. Gail and I were a bit shocked when Von asked what each of us wanted to eat, and Vikki said "lobster!" We had never been able to buy that, and even tried to get Vikki to change her order, but Von insisted that if she wants lobster... lobster she can have! This was a taste of what we would be able to do someday. Wow! We always thought it would be nice to go into a restaurant and order whatever your little heart desired and knew you could afford to pay for it....this would and did come true for us as time went by, just like Von had said! He was a wonderful and wise man and a great friend, and our hearts were so saddened when one day we heard he had had a heart attack while driving around on his routes in his Ford Edsel convertible. How blessed we had been to know this man. A man we will never forget!

I am racking my brain to know where to start on telling tales of our children. I guess the best place would be to start with the first child. Vikki Lynne Witte was born on July 23, 1951. She was the first baby girl born in the newly opened hospital in Jasper. It was a hot July, and on Sunday evening, July 22, 1951, we were playing cards at the home of Dr. Barrow and his wife Estelle, when Doc asked if we would like to drive to Jasper, IN for a Dairy Queen ice cream, fresh from the newly opened shop by Gail's cousins. Knowing that the hospital maternity floor was to open at 8:00 am the very next morning, at Jasper Memorial Hospital, the good doctor drove over to the hospital and rang a bell. When the nun came to answer his call, he told her he had a patient who was ready to have her baby and if she came early could he bring her in. The nun told him that it would be fine anytime during the night. The hospital officially opened at 8:00 am that morning and I checked in at 8:10. How's that for timing? I wasn't trying for a record of any kind. It was just time for our first baby to be born. Giving birth is not the easiest thing to do, and I soon found out that after the first one, they usually come quicker than the first one. Another lady came in at 9:00 and by 11 o'clock she had her third baby and it was a boy. In those days there was not a way to tell what gender your child would be before it was born, so since we had wanted a little girl, we prayed even harder to make ours a girl. Well, while the lady who got her birthing job done so quickly and was resting nicely in her room, I was still struggling, but finally at 5:15 that evening, our little princess made her appearance. Dr. Barrow referred to her as our little pullet. Do you know what a pullet is? It is a little chicken. But our little pullet didn't have feathers!!

So we had two distinctions...I was the first patient at the new hospital and we had the first baby girl! We stayed in the hospital for 4 days, and the other lady's husband had a garden, and he would bring fresh ear corn and green beans and since the maternity floor was the only floor officially open, she and I were the only patients in the entire hospital, we had the royal treatment and some delicious food. Time came for us to go home and a lot of things happened after that, but I want to jump ahead several years...let's see...it was actually 28 YEARS later. I decided to go to college and I was taking accounting and one day we had a shortage of books and were asked to share with someone. I sat next to a guy I had only seen in this class and one other that we both took, but I had never spoken to him. Being the interested and inquisitive person that I am, I asked his name. When he told me what it was, my mouth dropped open...almost to the floor, because I recognized that as the name of the little boy that was born on the same day as Vikki . I turned to him and repeated his name to him and he looked at me and said: "Are you the other lady?" When I told him that I was, we started talking and I pulled out a picture of Vikki, who by this time was around 28 years old. So the teacher asked if there was anything interesting going on that the class should know about, and I told him that there really was, and it was unbelievable. Who would have thought that after 28 years I would be sitting in a class room next to the boy who was born on the same day as my daughter... unbelievable, but interesting!

After Vikki was born in 1951, Rick was born in June of 1953, and then came Sarah in September, 1958, and a lot of good and not so good things happened while they were growing...so here we go...

I hardly know where to start on funny stories, but Vikki never did like going to sleep...we couldn't figure it out. My goodness, how much either of us would have loved to have a good night's sleep, but not our little night owl! I always loved to rock babies, so that part was not a problem. The problem came when Vikki went to sleep and I am thinking how good it is going to feel to get to bed...so I would ease out of my rocking chair and head for the bedroom to put my sleeping angel to bed, when two little eyes pop open and Vikki looks at me and says: "Wock me!" I knew that even though she didn't quite pronounce it right, she was NOT ready to go to bed...so it was back to the 'wocking' chair for another round of 'wocking'. She finally did fall asleep enough so I could lay her in her bed. This was an every night and every afternoon experience for what seemed like years. But as nature would have it, she finally grew up and things were almost normal.

Rick was born in Stork Hospital in Huntingburg (So named for Dr. Stork...not the bird!) on June 30, 1953, at five minutes to 9:00am. Gail was there and a few days later when he went on his sales route for the company he and is dad owned, he wrote a song to the tune 'Jimmy Cracked Corn'...and this is what he wrote:

"At five till nine last Tuesday morn,
A little son to us was born,
His hair is brown, his eyes are blue,
He tipped the scales at 9#2.
Oh, now the waiting time is done,
Jeannie's had a little son,
We're as proud as we can be,
Mommy, Daddy and Vikki!"

A hit song for sure!

There is one story I MUST tell about our baby boy, when one day while changing his diaper, low and behold, in that diaper was a $1o bill. I wiped my eyes and looked again with amazement...could it be?...

could we have a little boy that was comparing to the goose that laid the golden egg? I called his dad and said: "Sweetheart, you are not going to believe this but out son is cranking our ten dollar bills, so please go to the grocery and buy extra baby food"....WHOA...HOLD IT JUST A MINUTE!! At the beginning of my stories I said that all the stories I am writing are TRUE! Well, I have to confess that I only wish this one were true. It's not all false, because I did find a ten dollar bill in his diaper. But I soon found out it had fallen out of my shirt pocket. Oh my!!! I feel so much better with that confession! Had it been true, we would probably have made the 6 o'clock news. No. We just have a normal little boy.

With Vikki being two years older she wielded her authority like only an older sister can do. The kids had a wagon and how she kept from falling and injuring herself I can only imagine was due to guardian angels watching over my two little devils. In the wagon Vikki placed a chair and over the chair was the 'royal' wrap, (the blanket from her bed). She would sit on her 'throne' and command poor little Ricky to "PULL! She had some pretty harsh words for him if he didn't obey her commands, and I kept telling her to be careful what she did to her little brother, because someday he would grow up and just may beat the snot out of her! Enough for my advice! The rule of the 'queen' went on for a few months.

One day, Vikki decided to get into the paint. We were not real sure how she got it, but it must have come from Grandma Booty and Popo Jake's garage...they lived right next door to us... Anyway, I looked out the window and here came Vikki across the lawn with grey paint up to her elbows. I had no idea what to do with it! So I called her dad and he had to come home from work and help me clean her up and give her a bath and a lecture on the proper way to use paint...it was not body paint!

Dipping in the paint however, did not stop her from being the ever developing entrepreneur. She later went into the business of manufacturing perfume. She made one especially for me. She had taken a collection of my older perfumes and mixed them together and called her new concoction 'Lady of Dale'. What a delight to wear such an elegant fragrance!

The 'manufacturing plant' where this young entrepreneur was ever-expanding was none other than a deserted chicken house. Several years earlier this little wooden building that stood in our backyard had been home to several chickens. Having a concrete floor and openings in the back of the building made it ideal for youngsters to play without the fear of ruining anything, especially since the chickens were gone. We added some kitchen equipment to the furnishings in the chicken house, now renamed the play house... and provided many, many hours of entertainment not only to the girls but Rick even had a sleep over one night at least for part of the night. But his 'camping out' buddy felt the need to go home. We saw many mud pies, more perfume and some wonderful 'poison berry juice' come out of this wonderful place. Then one day when the kids had grown up and moved away, and he was thinking about retirement, Gail had a marvelous idea! He would change this little building into a workshop for himself, where he would be able to piddle around with something he had thought for a long time that he would like to try. So the little chicken house, turned play house turned into a nice little work shop.

The amazing thing was that not only did Gail find out the he liked wood working, he was pretty good at it and he started investing in some serious equipment and even attending classes in wood working. This little shop went on for a couple of years when one day he said he thought about enlarging it. He was also good at drawing up plans for things and he developed a great working area that was at least twice the size of the original building and he completed it with a front porch, to which Sarah and I added two old fashioned rocking chairs. Gail enjoyed his new hobby so much that after he retired I didn't see as much of him as I did when he went to work at the mill. Shortly after breakfast he would head for the shop, and I would have to call him in for lunch and often had to remind him it was dark and time to have dinner and go to bed! What a wonderful thing this came to be for him. He made a lot of nice furniture which family members and people around the area still have in their homes.

There is a funny story I must tell on him...I had asked him to build me one of those old fashioned garden swings. One that had two seats, facing each other, a slatted floor and overhead covering and you could sit and swing with a friend or all by yourself. The day came when his project was finished and I heard some unusual noise out toward the shop and when I looked, I saw a very perplexed husband, but he was laughing. It seems that he had built his project inside the shop but it was too big to go through the double doors so he had to dismantle his beautiful project and take it outside in smaller pieces. But, boy! Did we enjoy that swing!

There are so many funny, unusual, serious and sad stories I hope to get to tell you, and I will try to get to as many as I can, but I have an appointment with a doctor in Evansville, who is going to operate on my back, in the hopes of helping rid me of the pain I have all the time. He says the surgery is the only thing that will make me well, but he told me he is not sure I am strong enough to make it through the surgery, which is scheduled for April 3, 2014. But, like he said, this is the only way for me to have a chance to get better, and God and I have been through many, many frightening, life threatening situations, and He has always allowed me to come out on top. I am planning for another miracle. But should His choice be different this time, and He decides that it is time for me to go and live with Him until all of us get together again in heaven, I am not afraid. As a matter of fact, knowing that heaven is to be my ultimate home anyway, I might as well go see!

The surgery went well and I am much better thanks to a fantastic doctor.

In 2004 I had an abscess on my spine, which required a neurologist to fix. The abscess was caused because I was having so much back pain that I had to go to another doctor who would give me an injection directly into my back and that would relieve the pain for a few months. For a couple of years I had been going to <u>Welborn </u>Clinic where I had two_really nice young doctors who gave me the injections. But, unfortunately, Welborn Clinic closed and I had to go to a Dr. at Deaconess Hospital. Dr. 'NO_NO' was a red-headed Irishman that for some reason, I didn't like very much when I first met him. He came to my room and talked with me a bit before I was taken to the room where he would give me the injection. My sense of not liking the man was right on. While he was supposed to be paying very close attention to me, his patient, instead he was cracking jokes with the 2 nurses in the room. Remember, this is a very delicate procedure and his full attention should have been only on what he was doing to me. In a few minutes he told me to let him know if I felt any pain. Just about the time he said the words, I felt a pain and said so. Now he did what he should NEVER have done! He pulled the needle just far enough out of my back to allow bacteria into my body. When I recovered and was ready to go home, I could not stand on my own. The nurse who was with me as I was leaving the hospital had to help me to a wheel chair. By the time we got to the car where Gail was waiting to drive me home, I was afraid to try to stand, but I made it!! Usually it takes a few days...no more than 4 or 5 to feel the healing effects of the procedure; however, I didn't get better. I called the doctor and he said I should not be concerned and just wait a few more days. But I did not get better in over a week. Then one day I went to Kathy for a body massage, and became so ill she had to have her husband, Howard, drive me home, and she followed to be with me and to take her husband back to her shop. They called Gail and we went to the emergency room at Deaconess and I was given several tests, one of which was an MRI that evidently gives a very in- depth image of what is going on inside, and WOW!...they found I had an abscess on my spine, which meant I needed surgery ASAP, or run the risk of being paralyzed or even death. My neurologist who would do the surgery was Dr. David. I did not know him personally, but his father was the pastor of a little church in Louisville, KY where Vikki attended. Gail and I always went there when we visited Vikki, and later when Sarah lived there, she also attended. The pastor and his wife often stopped by our house on their way to visit their son Dr. David in Evansville...so I knew *of* the good Dr. and figured that as much as we loved and respected his parents, he must be a good guy. I was admitted to the hospital and placed in a room directly by the nurse's station, where they would come and visit with me often. I realized later that they were watching for signs of my getting worse or worse yet, starting to become paralyzed, which is exactly what happened about 5am on Friday. My surgery was scheduled for Monday morning; however, all of a sudden my room was full of nurses, my primary doctor, Dr. A. was there and very soon, my

Dr. E, with his cell phone to his ear, was barking orders and at the same time wheeling me toward the surgery room. What had happened was that when the nurse came in around 5am to check on me, she had me do the simple test of pulling my toes up, then pushing them down and I did it!! At least I thought I had done it, but not so.

That is when all the commotion began…I had started the paralysis and they all got in a 'hurry-up' mode. I remember Dr. E. calling for the anesthesiologist who was still in bed when he called. Later the doctor told me that had they waited another hour, I would have been totally paralyzed. But this surgery was very much a success. This started in February 2004 and the surgery was in April, after which I had to make daily trips to the hospital for about 6 weeks for intravenous medicine. This process took about 2 hours daily, including Sunday. Gail was so good about taking care of me.

It was also at this time that Justin & Elana were planning to be married. The wedding day came on May 8th and I wouldn't have missed that for anything…but I was so weak I could barely walk and I could't even go to the wedding reception. But I do remember what a beautiful wedding it was. Justin looked so proud as he stood on the stage of the outdoor Lincoln Amphitheater waiting for his bride who was standing at the top of the facility with many steps to come down to get to where Justin and the wedding party was waiting. I remember looking back at Elana when she was waiting with her dad, Kenny, to start her walk, and thought she had to be the prettiest bride EVER!!

It was at this time that I had to start wearing a wig. When I went to the hospital for my daily dose of antibiotics, I had what is called a 'pick line'(sp?) in my arm. They did that so they wouldn't have to stick me every day. All they had to do was hook up the medicine to the contraption already in my arm, and that wasn't so bad. But I couldn't reach up to take care of my own hair, so I asked a lady at the hospital where I could find something to cover my head so I wouldn't look ridiculous out in public. She told me about the wig shop and I went with the intention of getting some kind of scarf to put over my hair, but Anne, the lady at the wig shop, brought out a wig and put it on my and I was hooked on the wigs forever. Gail even said it was one of the greatest things because like most everyone else, I had not just a bad hair day occasionally, but now it was every day, but the wig solved the problem and my hair always looked nice.

The story about the back surgery in 2004 opens the door for the second back surgery in 2014...10 years later...almost to the day! Both were in early April. The second back surgery came as a result of a knee replacement by a doctor that I really liked as a person, but evidently he didn't do what he should have, and since he did the knee replacement in 2010, I have had problems with pain and inability to walk without assistance. But when I kept on with the pain after the knee surgery, Dr. B. said he wanted to have my back Xrayed. The Xray revealed what he thought was the problem... the L4 and L5 discs in my lower back were way out of alignment and would require surgery to fix. He said I would need to see a neurosurgeon...well, I had no problem naming...no..., INSISTING, on Dr. E.

When I took the Xrays of my back to Dr. E., he agreed that my back was in trouble and it could only be corrected with surgery, but he said he couldn't do it. I asked him why and he simply said to me: "Because you won't make it, and I don't like to lose a patient." Sarah was with me in his office and she knew how I felt about going into dangerous territory... why not...I had been there before, so I told Dr. E., I wouldn't take his 'no' for an answer, because it didn't matter to me whether I came through the surgery fine and came home and got back to 'normal', or if I would just slip off during the surgery and go to my eternal home to be with God...I was ready!!! He left his room giving orders to others in the office as to how to set things in motion for my next adventure under the knife.

Knowing that I just might not come back to live with Kenny & Sarah in Santa Claus, where I had been for 3 years, I prepared for departing this life by making my funeral arrangements...why not...I didn't want the family having to make last minute decisions and sometimes wonder if I would have approved of what they did, so I did it myself; however, again, with the 2 best physicians, I made it. The day of the surgery, Vikki, Rick and Sarah were with me, along with a pastor from my church and his wife. I had chosen the proper one to preach my funeral, if necessary. We all met in a little room where we talked together, and prayed together ...even laughed a bit, then I was off to the OR (operating room). While I was waiting for the Dr. E., I told those who were in the OR at the time, how I felt about what was about to happen to me, and told them not to be upset if I left them right in the middle of the surgery...I was not afraid!! And honestly, I was a bit surprised when I woke up still in the hospital. Recovery this time was very easy and fast, but I still have the frustration of having had the knee surgery which should have given me a better leg to walk on, but instead I have been left with pain and being somewhat incapacitated.

As I got better and felt I was able to pretty well take care of myself, Kenny and Sarah had decided they wanted to downsize their beautiful home. Since I was ready and excited to be more independent once again Sarah and I started checking out places, then Rick told us about Lake Side Manor where several people from our church were living. After Sarah and I came and took a tour, it was easy to make the decision to move to 3531 Turtle Dove Court in Evansville where I am at the present time, and love my apartment and my independence.

Let's go back and let me tell you more of my adventures as a parent of 3 totally different children.

I told you about Vikki and the paint, also about the homemade perfume, and her ability to manipulate her little brother, but she also had some hidden talents. Gail and I were always interested in watching for whatever signs we could see of anything we thought our first child might be gifted with. It so happened that Gail's sister, Fae, came from California to visit and she taught Vikki a bit about playing the guitar, enough so that Vikki decided she would like to learn to play well, so that Christmas Gail and I gave her her first guitar. The amazing thing about her playing was that she taught herself by spending a lot of time in her room listening to music and playing along with it. She developed her own unique way of playing and she played the notes to the music, not just the chords. By the time she was about 17, she got a job playing her guitar and singing at the Holiday Inn in Jasper. She was too young to perform in the bar, so she entertained the crowds in the dining room. I remember many nights she would come home and shake her guitar and watch the $$$ fall out from the tips peoples gave her. She went on to accompany the swing choir at school and from there she spent probably 20 years singing and playing in hotel lounges. After she had been playing for quite a while she decided she should take some lessons. LOL!! They were definitely beneficial, because she just kept improving. Over several years she played in hotel lounges and even on the riverboat. I think she is still playing with some of her old music buddies occasionally. And of course, she grew up, got married... several times...but we don't talk about that much, because she is currently married to a wonderful man and seems very happy as she is now getting about old enough to retire...OH! MY! WHERE DID THE TIME GO?? Yes she worked other jobs, mainly in helping people understand the harmful effects of using drugs...the damage it can do to your health as well as the high cost of the drugs. And sadly many of her 'patients' ended up in the hospital, and some even took their own lives. I know there were some success stories, but it is a sad thing to have to deal with. Oh, yes, she also had a son in 1985, Jonathan. He is now living in Louisville. And Vikki and Mike have moved to Jeffersonville, IN.

As for Rick, remember the little song I told you Gail wrote about him? See, music just keeps popping up in our family, and Rick turned out to be exceptionally musically talented. He learned to play the piano by listening to the theme songs of TV shows when he was about 5 years old. At that time the TV set was in the living room as well as the piano. I contacted a teacher in Tell City to get him into lessons, because I wanted him to learn how to read the notes. He didn't stay with the piano lessons much longer than I did back when I tried. Only difference, he could really make some pretty good music and he had the talent to memorize and even to write music. When he was in the 5th grade it was time to decide what instrument he wanted to play in the band...he chose the trumpet. Oh, yes, and Vikki played the clarinet. I forgot to tell you about the band Vikki and Rick were both in. They called it the "5 Hits and a Miss"...there were 5 guys and Vikki...pretty neat wasn't it?

After the little band of 5 hits and a Miss was winding down, or maybe it was going on at the same time...it was a few years ago and my memory isn't what it used to be. That's why I'm working on this project as fast as I can. LOL !! But, as I started to say...Rick and a few of his other musically talented friends formed their own band. It was a time when a guy named Herb Alpert was very popular with his brass band.

These kids were about 14 -15 years old. Honestly, those guys were so good they sounded just like ole Herbie himself. As a matter of fact there was a talent show at our school and Vikki played guitar and sang, Rick and the boys did their brass band thingy and there were a few other talent acts, and even Sarah got in the act, by, of all things, doing a very exotic dance, complete with black lace stockings and all…and she was about a 4th grader…Vikki won, the brass boys were second, another band was third and we were told afterward that Sarah was very much in the running for the third place spot, but the judges were seeing a pattern of 'Witte's' on stage and did what they thought was best. And as things often go, the father of one of the girl singers followed us to our car and had a few choice words for us, as if we had done the judging!!! Well… facts are facts, and thankfully the talent didn't stop there. Many times I would go outside our house when one group or the other was practicing, and just listen with a very thankful heart that music was filling their time rather than many other things that would not be good for them. And I would think that as long as I live, I can always remember the sounds of talent and very good music coming from our home…and still often relive some of those times.

Rick had so much musical talent in his body that he would try to make music out of most anything he could find. I had a portable hand mixer with a ten speed dial on top, and along with Rick's musical talent, he also loved to bake. He worked at Dale State Bank in the summer, on his break from Indiana University, and enjoyed making 'goodies' to take to work. Sooooo, one day he was mixing brownies with the little ten speed portable mixer, and I guess he recognized that each setting on the dial made a different tone, so, here I am off in another room of the house when I hear my electric mixer playing "On Top Of Old Smoky". There goes my talented son, I thought with a smile, only to learn that in another effort to fix something for the workers at the bank, Rick was going to bake a cake, and decided the try the theme from the movie Exodus, and sad to say, he ruined the cake by over mixing it, and I have forgotten whether he was able to finish his musical effort or not. I often told him that he saved the family a lot of money because we had a built in home entertainment!

He had a record player and his Aunt Fae had subscribed to the 'record a month' club. He received records (78rpm discs) in the mail. The records had different stories on them and if I was working in the kitchen, he would bring his record player where I was and sit and listen to his stories. He really was great company for me while Gail was at work and Vikki at school, and Sarah usually sleeping, but some of this was before she was born. He was an 'A' student in school and won every music award available, even a commendation from the United States Marine Corps Band!

He enjoyed building model rockets that you could even launch. He launched several from our back yard. Then one day after he had built his biggest rocket...I have forgotten the name of it...but it was big and very nice, so rather than just launch it the same way he did his others, he went to the Mill and built a unique aluminum box that had 4 launch buttons on it, toggle switches, and a key fixture to turn that part on, it also required being attached to a car battery and then he was ready to go. This was a beautiful launch that ended up on a hill several blocks away in the St Joe Catholic Church parking lot. We thought if he did anything like that again, we might have to get clearance from the FAA, so he wouldn't bump into any aircraft that happened to be flying over!

I think he really liked his little sister, because one night we didn't know where he was. Our search took us to the bedroom where Sarah was sleeping, and there he was, underneath her crib, in his pj's, reading her a story by the night light.

Yea, he learned to 'read' early. He wasn't actually reading, but speaking what he had heard read to him enough times that he memorized the book. When Vikki was in Mrs. Livengood's second grade, I was room mother. One day I decided to take Rick to let him 'read' to the second grade class. Mable Roell was his first grade teacher-in-waiting, and she came to hear him 'read'. His favorite book was about a pony called Jim Jump. As Mrs. Roell watched as he 'read', she later asked Mrs. Livengood if she had any suggestions as to what to do with a child who was already doing what was her job as a teacher.

Rick often called his Aunt Sadie who lived only a few blocks away, to see if he could go to her house to spend the night. Of course Aunt Sadie was thrilled to have him come to spend the night, especially in the summer when she was not teaching. I would pack his small overnight case and unbeknownst to him, I watched from a safe distance behind until I saw he made safe contact with Aunt Sadie. He had often dialed her telephone number, but one night I overheard him sounding frustrated. When I went closer, I heard the reason. He evidently had dialed the wrong number, at least a couple of times, at which point the telephone operator would advise him to hang up and try again. My persistent little guy was very accommodating, but before the third attempt, he told the operator, and I quote his very words: "OK, but this time DON'T YOU ANSWER!"

One other time I remember so well. We had open burning in Dale, and in the fall we had fun raking and burning leaves, but we also had an open barrel we used for burning trash. This is also at the time we had a collie fenced in in our back yard. This collie was part of the family and even sported an insulated doghouse. One day Rick had some reason to be playing with a broom. Since his grandmother had recently burned her papers in the barrel, Rick started poking at the remnants of the fire with a straw broom. When he found out it was a bit difficult to put the fire out that had caught the broom, Rick decided the best place to beat the fire out must be the doghouse! NOT!! Now we had another problem…putting out a fire in a doghouse, which we successfully did.

Rick's love for me came one time in the form of a hand written note which stated: "To my mommy." And inside this sweet note was a large dead dragon fly, signed: "Your loveable son Ricky". I still have the note, but somewhere over the years the already dead dragon fly got lost. I don't think a more heartfelt love could possibly be shown. These are things a mother can never forget. It is things like this that makes parenting worth it!

Child #3…Sarah Jean, born September 21, 1958 at Huntingburg hospital, at a time when new mothers still stayed in the hospital for 5 days. Before I start telling tales on her, I want you to know that God never created a sweeter child. When Rick started to school a year after she was born, my days were heaven.

When Sarah was in the eighth grade her dad took her to a small town in Illinois to purchase a horse. We had a friend, Leon Zimmer, who raised horses and his wife, Mary, gave riding lessons, so we were all set. Except when they arrived to pick up the horse, which she called 'Flame', he had stepped in a hole left by the winter's freezing and thawing, and injured his ankle. She was told she would not be able to ride him until his ankle healed. She was very patient with the process and never fussed about having to treat his wound or clean his stable. She always took him a treat of apples or carrots, and yes, there was an early bond between girl and horse.

It took Flame's ankle several weeks to heal and Sarah was ready for some lessons in riding and caring for the present love of her life. She would spend hours riding. This was at the time our collie was only a pup, and boy was he smart, too! One day Sarah rode Flame to the house and 'Laddie', the collie, was running around outside his pen. He immediately ran to Sarah who was still mounted on the horse, and when I tried to get the dog, feeling he might not be safe around the horse, that smart little collie planted himself firmly between the hind legs of the horse. No way was I going to retrieve that puppy from his chosen place of hiding. But no harm came to him and often when he grew up, he accompanied Sarah on her rides. We also owned a cute little Peek-a-poo, named Merf. Now Merf, Laddie, Flame and Sarah all got along quite well, and it was quite a sight to see Sarah on her horse galloping down the road, with Laddie pretty much able to keep up, and poor little Merf doing the best he could to stay up with his friends. But he soon had to come home and rest. Sarah had a friend who also loved to go horseback riding, and she and Dave Hile made good use of the new roadbed that was soon to be I64, just north of Dale.

Then one day my back doorbell rang. After they rang doorbell several times, I felt surely something was wrong and went as fast as I could to find two young men holding Sarah between them. When she didn't look hurt I asked them in to explain. It seems Sarah, along with her faithful companion, Flame, had been out riding with these friends and she had to jump a ditch.

According to Sarah, she had to dismount in order to cross the creek. She slipped just as Flame jumped and he landed on the back of her legs. We took her to the hospital to check her out and found that she only suffered bruises to both calves of her legs, with the imprint of horse hooves very visible. I asked her what she thought when she saw this huge animal flying over her. These are her exact words: "Mom, I thought: What a beautiful jump!"

I personally love horses, but only to look at. And the horse knows I am intimidated by him. The day I decided to ride Sarah's beautiful Flame, I could almost hear the horse laugh. And he took me straight to our big cedar tree and tried his best to rub me off. One trip around the cedar tree was enough for me, so I said: "Okay big fella...you win!!"

Four years later Sarah left for college and Gail took on the responsibility of Flame. About a year later he told Sarah he just didn't have time to care for Flame properly and he felt we should try to find someone who would buy him. He found a good home and we all had had our fun with the horse.

It was August 1979 and Gail decided to take the whole family to a Dude Ranch in Colorado. Our family now included Rick's wife. They had just gotten married. What a great time we had. And then the day came to go on a trail ride.

Me & 'Big Ben'

Everyone was excited but me. I decided I would stay behind and let the rest of them have this experience. But they would have none of it…I needed to go on the trail ride with them! My horse's name was Big Ben. Almost enough said!! I am barely over 5' tall, and weighed more than I wanted to, and I felt a problem coming on. How in the world was I going to mount this giant of a horse. Our guide's name was Gray, a real cowboy, one who actually rode the cattle trails from Texas to Montana. He came up with an idea. Put the horse in the ditch and I would be much closer to the saddle…ha…ha…ha! It worked and I had mounted my steed and was ready to hit the trail…we have a picture to prove it, but it will NOT go into this book. This was a ride none of us could forget. I am on this huge animal and we are riding up switchbacks, where the horse crosses one hoof over the other…why, you ask? Because we are riding straight up a cliff and rocks are breaking loose on the side of the 'Mount Everest' and tumbling into the 'mile deep lake' below. I expected to be dumped off any minute, but Big Ben had other ideas. We reached the top and boy did I enjoy the break, and then we had to come back down 'Mount Everest' the same way we went up. Unfortunately when we had reached a flat space near home base when Big Ben reared up and dumped me on the hard ground. Believe it or not, I landed between two huge rocks and wasn't sure I could get up. Gray had ridden ahead of us because the ride was almost over. Someone rode ahead and Gray came back in his truck to pick up his less than accomplished rider. Later, back at the cabin, my backside began to swell up, then turn blue and then assorted other colors. My entire family wanted a chance to see what we all dubbed my 'Picasso'. I couldn't fasten my jeans for several days. My son-in-law even took a picture and…it was the only one on that roll of film that didn't print out!! I thank my lucky stars for that! Sorry to throw this in the midst of Sarah's story, but it just seemed appropriate.

Sarah was also a Jr. High cheer leader and we had a big Buick and often when the cheer team and friends wanted to go to the ball game, we just filled that ole Buick to capacity. We had fun.

She, like Vikki and Rick played in the band. Rick played a trumpet and Vikki & Sarah each played the clarinet, as I stated earlier.

"Spirit of '76 Singers"

Sarah's class had several girls who were really good singers, and since they were going to graduate in 1976, and there were 12 girls they called themselves "The Spirit of '76". Let's see if I can remember them all...there was Sarah, of course, then Michelle Kirby, Pat Schum, Jane Hufnagel, Maureen Meyer, Kelley Snow, Rita Hagedorn, Marsha Wedeking, Jane Hufnagel, Linda Rickelman, Kris Hunter, Donna Gessner and Sarah Witte.. They sang at several events at school; they sang at their swim coaches wedding (Gayle Zion was the daughter of Congressman & Mrs. Roger Zion of Evansville), for a Girl Scout Jamboree; went to Indianapolis to sing for a veterans group, and were in the Evansville Freedom Festival parade and met with Mayor Russel Lloyd and Senator Dick Lugar. They also sang for President Gerald Ford who also came to Evansville. Guess who organized and directed them???? Sarah's brother, Rick! Rick had a helper, too, in Warren Dressler. Rick played guitar when they were in the proper places and Warren played piano for the more formal events. A few of the mothers were interested in helping and we bought material for a couple of different outfits. One was a red skirt with a red, white and blue elastic waist band. They wore white shirts and red or blue vests upon which one gifted mother embroidered 'Spirit of '76', and they all wore the same style white shoes. The outfits they wore on the float in the Freedom Festival parade were summery white with each dress being white and having red or blue polka dots, very fitting since the festival was in the summer. In the winter, I wrote the mayor's office to get permission for the girls to sing Christmas songs on the Walkway in downtown Evansville, and they wore blue jeans, white turtle neck shirts and red sweatshirts with a big '76' on the front. Since I didn't know where to get enough real red sweatshirts I had Rick get them at Indiana University, where he was in school. It always makes me happy to go back in my memory and think of the wonderful moments I had the pleasure of listening to the music my children have given me. There are probably a lot of times I have missed telling about each one of the kid's accomplishments, but then, again, I could probably make this entire story about their music. I remember one night when the '76er's' were practicing in our living room, I went out on our front side walk and just stood, thanking God for what I was hearing and asking that it be embedded in my heart and mind always.

But surely there is more to tell about Sarah and her adventures, so I will start digging in my brain and see what I can find, because I feel certain you guys want to hear some more about her mishaps, but before I do I want to tell you about some more of the outside help I had with these 12 girls. When they were invited to be in the Freedom Festival parade, there was work to do, and it was amazing how everything just fell in place when anybody connected with it gave so willingly. First I had to get a wagon. We have many farmers around Dale, and all I had to do was ask. Got the wagon...now how are we going to get it to move in the parade...I surely can't pull the ole thing, so I asked a friend whom I worked with on the Dale Fall Festival, and we decided that his pick-up truck would be better that a tractor, because some tractors are a bit loud and the girls would be singing...now what do we add that will perk up the looks of the farm wagon? I honestly do not remember how we put anything on the base of the wagon, because we also needed some way to support the girls while riding, or else we would just have a pile of girls on a wagon trying to sing, as Rick would be struggling to keep the guitar and the girls together...another problem to solve! This is where my husband came in, and I'm not sure what he made for them, but he was always able to create something out of whatever he would find around the mill or maybe he would check with one of the merchants in town for assistance, but all I know is the girls and Rick had support while moving very well along the parade route. But the float just wasn't quite yet finished, so I went to Heritage Hills High School to check with the Art teacher, Mr. Morrison, for some ideas. Wallah!! (Is that how you spell it?) Here is what we did...I purchased canvas from a man I knew who did upholstering, my husband again came up with exactly what else I needed...a piece of metal tubing that could be bent and fastened onto the wagon, the canvas was sewn to fit the tubing and the art class did an outstanding job of painting the canvas. It displayed 13 white stars on a blue background and in the center, as big as it could be painted to fit were the numbers'76, and also sported 13 red and white stripes, ala Betsy Ross, created by Heritage Hills Art class!! What had started out as a hair-brained idea had ended up involving several people in the community and presenting a neat looking float!! So don't ever think something is impossible!

I found that Sarah had developed a talent for counselling as early as first grade. It was just a thing she could do. And she did it all through school. Afterwards, she developed a love for learning scripture and began seriously studying the Word of God, to the point that I even bought her a book on the Hebrew language. When she was attending Dale Bible Church, she and another lady 'Carole Briscoe' decided to do jail ministry together. Every Tuesday evening for several years these two ladies would head to the Warrick County Jail and teach a bible lesson to the women there. Now Warrick County was not a women's jail even though there were women there, so Sarah and Carole were escorted each week by the jailer to the women's cell and were locked in with the women while they had their lesson. I asked her if she was ever afraid to do this and she said ABSOLUTELY NOT! She saw these women as mothers, sisters, daughters and friends who had encountered some hardships and needed Jesus. She loved what she was doing so much that she developed a ministry called 'Bridge Builders'. It was a way of helping these women regain a path back into society. She had cards made up with her name and a number on it so once these ladies had served their time, and if they wanted to continue bible study, they knew how to reach her. One Sunday as Sarah and her family were leaving church she got a call from one of these sweet ladies. Her name is Evette. I don't know all the details, but apparently she had spent the night in a dumpster at the Eastland mall in Evansville and was feeling down on her luck. Needless to say Sarah headed for Evansville. Evette had been separated form her family , who lived in Louisville, for several years and had gotten her life in a bit of a mess. After a long day of counseling, the two had dinner and picked up a few essentials at Walmart. They prayed together and Sarah headed home. A few days later Sarah received a call from Evette, thanking her for the time they had spent together and to say she had returned home to her family who had been praying for her. What a happy ending. Another very special gal who's name is Jasmine, also had a hard time with a happy ending. She had met Sarah in Warrick County jail, but had gone on to serve tome time in Rockville prison. She and Sarah wroth letters back and forth while she was in Rockville and the day she got out she called Sarah and they continued to meet for a couple of years. Jasmine ended up graduating college and worked her way back to a good clean life. She continued to grow in her faith and invited Sarah to attend her baptism at Bethel Church in Evansville. I know every story she had with these women didn't always have such a happy ending but some did. She loved serving others in this way. I'm not at all surprised that one of her daughters 'Autumn' wanted to go into full time missions. Actually all three of the girls are serving the Lord in some way and I could not be more blessed. Sarah worked at the Dale Pharmacy for a time. She put her Biblical learning into practice in her everyday life, when one day one of her co-workers, Kelly Jones, asked her to help her in understanding the scriptures and how they changed her life. She met with Kelly privately and afterwards Kelly asked if she could visit Sarah again and bring a friend. Friends kept telling friends and soon Sarah was teaching Bible study classes in her home on a weekly basis. The group has been as large as twelve, but it varies with people's other responsibilities and time schedules. I was also the welcome recipient of these classes since this was shortly after Gail passed away and I was living with Kenny and Sarah. We also welcomed a friend into the class who soon became an extension of our family. Karen Claise is a nurse practitioner who was going through some rough times and welcomed the introduction to Sarah's study group. Several of these ladies have taken advantage of Sarah's counseling ability.

Sarah has another knack, too. If she wanted something badly enough, she went after it. This next adventure of hers began when she decided to move to Florida. My brother Harvle and his wife Corrine lived in Clearwater and had said that she was welcome to come and stay with them until she could make it on her own. She had always said that one thing she could never do was become a waitress.

But in a place like Clearwater, Fl., you would probably become a waitress, or starve! Sure enough she got a job at a Holiday Inn on the beach. When she was making enough money to afford her own apartment she met a girl who lived in her same complex and also worked at the same Holiday Inn as food and beverage director. Sarah had found that the fastest way to make money was to work in the coffee shop, but as she began watching the food and beverage director she decided that she wanted to move up a bit. She worked her way up to hostess by way of the kitchen and the bar, but she still wanted to be food and beverage director. So when your goal is seemingly beyond your reach, what should you do?

Why not go to your boss with a cockamamie story that comes straight from your own fertile brain and tell him that you want to move to Ft. Lauderdale where you understand the boss there is looking to hire. Before long she was packing her bags and moving to Ft. Lauderdale. Before you could count to three, she was in the boss's office in Ft. Lauderdale telling him that she had been sent there from Clearwater to work in the new program he has. The boss, not wanting to be caught up in something he knew *nothing* about and in order to speed things along, asked Sarah just how she understood the program would work. Without hesitation, Sarah laid out the entire plan to the boss and he told her she could start right away with 3 months in the kitchen, 3 months in the bar, 3 months as hostess and 3 months in the accounting department. Can you imagine anyone pulling off a stunt such as this? I guess there was nothing really wrong with what she did, and she achieved her goal, and later was assigned to a Holiday Inn in Louisville, KY as *assistant food and beverage director*...she almost achieved her dream. She was close enough and enjoyed it, and I was so glad to have her back closer to home!

I must interject a vital point here! I grew up in a family that sang together, cried together and did a whole lot of hugging, then married into a family that NEVER touched each other, except in the case of a time when I spanked one or all three of the kids. Then the emotions ran something like this...the kids cried from the spanking, I cried because the dog took a nip at me for spanking her kids!!! Now that's emotions to write home about!! But honestly, deep down, I miss the days of hugs. I was thrilled when once we had a pastor at our church who always announced from the pulpit as he ended his Sunday morning message with: 'Hugs in the back'! I always liked him.

But when I think about the time the dog took a nip at me I recall how the nuns who were teaching at the Catholic school across the street from where we lived, and how they took to our dog. Her name was Toodles and she guarded the kids when they were out at play, but she also became connected to the nuns because they feed her. As a matter of fact she began gaining so much weight I wrote a limerick about her that went like this:

> There once was a dog named Toodles
> Who loved to eat beef and noodles.
> She ate and she ate with no thought of her weight,
> And now there is oodles of Toodles.

The nuns loved Toodles so much that if the kids came around, the nuns introduced our kids as Toodles kids'!

How about another interesting float that was another miracle?

I don't remember if I ever told you of an honor I had in the community of Dale, but in November 1967, a friend of mine and a little red-headed guy named Bob Davis known by everybody and was very much into doing anything for our community, and was so patriotic, he told me he bled red, white and blue! Bob called me one day and asked if I would serve on the steering committee in starting a true Dale Fall Festival. Over the years different organizations and church groups had tried at making a Fall Festival work, but when it didn't happen, Bob decided maybe it would be better if we put together a festival that involved all aspects of the community. So in November 1967, there were 5 people, including Bob that set about the task of uniting the community with a real community effort. The others on the committee were Benno Schum, Abie Lovell, Norma Ficker and me. I will tell you now that we must have done a bang up job because the Dale Fall Festival is still a much looked forward event in our community and this is 2019. Before I go further, I have to tell you that our Vikki was the first Fall Festival Queen, crowned in Sept, 1968. I may tell you more about the festival later, but I must get back to the story about the float, which was connected with the festival.

How this next adventure started, I do not recall, but I knew the Lincoln Boyhood National Memorial superintendent, Al Banton, quite well. On the grounds of the park is a replica of the cabin where Abraham Lincoln studied law by candle light the several years he lived right in Spencer County, and daily there were people playing the parts of the people who would have been around the cabin at Abe's time. They did household chores, had animals, and even grew a garden from seeds that were used also at Abe's time. One day I was talking with a lady who worked at the cabin and an idea cropped into my head. With all this beautiful history right here in our front yard, why not do something with it. I knew I would need backing so I pitched the idea to the Fall Festival group and was given the go ahead; however, with the people on the committee business people I was left to my own devices to put my plan into action. When I talked to Superintendent Al Banton, he liked the idea I had, which was "Christmas In The Cabin". The lady at the Abe Lincoln cabin was named Mary Cohen and she and a group of people had Abe's cabin running much as in Abe's day throughout the summer months for the public to enjoy. When I spoke to her about my idea, she told me she and her brother had a 'cut-away-cabin' they had used at a flower show in Chicago a few years before, and it was just right for our float. The cabin exceeded my expectations, in that not only was it cut away on the sides, but the inside had been painted by a local artist with a fire place a rug and some other décor that fit the room. Mr. Banton was so excited about the cabin, he decided he would 'borrow' one of the park trucks and mount this on its flat bed. By now things were heating up, and, as usual, I didn't do very many things that I didn't manage to get my husband involved in. Thankfully, he was not only good about going along with my exuberant ideas, but he usually became very involved. At least as much as his work duties would allow.

The parade was in the fall and we could enter the float in the WROZ radio station's Christmas parade which was held in November.

At this point, I had to start some of our 'footwork'. I thought: "What can we use as a base for the house, so I called a company who provided the imitation grass for funeral sites, and simply asked if they would have enough for us to borrow some for our needs, and their answer was "yes"! Then, by this time Mr Banton was all in and he told me that since this parade we were planning to be in was after the park closed for the summer, he would grant us permission to use ANY of the furnishings in the real cabin to dress up our cut-away for the float. So now we have a cabin and furnishings. Now if it is Christmas, we have to have a Christmas tree. Again Mr. Banton went above and beyond his duty to see that we had whatever we needed. But we just couldn't find a proper size tree, so now it's time for Gail to help out. He came down to the garage in the park where we were working and found that there were two spindly cedars close by, that if tied together would make a good enough Christmas tree, but we needed a sturdy base for it to sit in,,,after all, it will be riding through the streets of Evansville, which just might get bumpy, so meanwhile back at the Mill with Gail, where he found an iron circle of some kind with a hole in the middle, and we were sure the tree wouldn't go any place in this thing. One of our committee members, Benno Schum, heard about this and said something to his wife, who just happened to have a box of imitation gingerbread men as well as a few ornaments that would have come straight out of the era we were dealing with. We knew that the tree décor would not be complete without strings of cranberries and popcorn. We had a 'work' session at my house one evening and soon we had the tree taken care of. It was perfect...now there were a couple of other things we needed...people...who will be the 'family' in the cabin? Mrs. Banton and her daughter Susan, volunteered, along with another young girl, Pam Stechmann....now we need a 'father figure'. One easily came to mind...Larry Schnuck!! He would be perfect as he lived in Lincoln City, practically across from Abe's place, and he certainly looked the part...tall, lean, and a willing volunteer and he just happened to own a musket!! Now we are about to outgrow our space on the truck bed, so Mr. Banton added a platform that would be the perfect place for Larry to stand as if looking for game, maybe!

O.K. now we have the main part of the truck finished and I figured the rest of the finishing touches would be up to my fertile brain, which by now was running on all cylinders. The funeral grass covered the floor area and hung down on the sides of the truck, which made the perfect place to identify what we had. I love doing this stuff, and decided I would print the words "Christmas in the Cabin" on either side of the float. In trying to figure out what to use for lettering, I remembered our local doctor, Dr. Barrow, who had tongue depressors in a jar in his office. Since I am no stranger to asking for thing, I asked and Dr. Barrow freely gave! These tongue depressors were exactly the size I needed and could easily make a readable sign...white letters trimmed in black against the green grass...PERFECT!

Done? Not quite! It seemed to me that in most parades there were banner carriers preceding the float...another challenge, but again, all the help I needed as well as another use for the tongue depressors. I purchased a brass curtain rod, some black felt material, some white fringe and two girls, Jenny Wahl and Pam Wynn, who just happened to fit into the black sequined uniforms of our high school majorettes. Their sign simply said "Dale, Indiana"! Now are we ready to go?? We have the float on the truck bed along with the extra platform.

We have all the décor and family members, and our 2 girls

announcing where we were from, so let's go! But we have to get this float to Evansville the night before so we can speed down Saturday morning.

We had a wake-up call for 4 AM. But I have another problem. Vikki had been away at college but got sick and had to come home and she was in the hospital with a tonsillectomy, and I wanted to be there with her. Her dad had gone up earlier, but since he had to go to work the next day, I got night watch!

Friday evening, Mr. Banton drove the truck and I drove my car behind him, and just out of Boonville...this was before I-64...I could see something slipping, and figured we were just going to end up spilling part of the float in Boonville, so we pulled over tied it down better and away we went. My thoughts at this point were: 'We look like the Beverly Hillbillies, and I don't care if the ole thing does fall apart, because...I just don't care...I have to go to the hospital.' We made it to Evansville and got our spot to park and be prepared to unfold and spruce it up the next morning. I got to the hospital and sat with Vikki until 2 AM, and decided I had better get home and in bed because I had to get up in 2 hours. I bought a package of cinnamon rolls and got a strong cup of coffee in hopes of deterring sleep until after the parade, but I crashed and thought at the time that I didn't really care whether or not I got up at 4...but I slept, and woke up at exactly 4am, got dressed, headed out to pick up the marching girls, then meet at Banton's place and get on with it...but Larry Schnuck overslept. But the fact that we got started a bit later than we had planned was soon erased by the fact that this 'provider-father-figure' had made arrangements with a man we knew who lived on the way down who raised quail and checkers. Chuckers are a good bit larger than quail, and we put two live birds cage in my car and kept them there until we knew our float was ready and we got into our position in the parade line-up. At the proper time, Larry wrung the necks of the chuckers which gave them the appearance of just having been shot with his trusty musket.

Away we went, and I left to go to the reviewing stand, where I had convinced the president of our town board, Jim Wetzel, that he MUST be there to show as much of our community spirit as possible. Other places had their mayors, but town board president was as close as we came. As the float went moving along, I prayed that the ole thing would at least stay together for the length of the parade, and then let us go home...I AM TIRED!!

The sun was shining. This was a beautiful crisp cold November morning and I watched with a bit of pride, along with all my other feelings, and surprisingly, the entire group on the reviewing stand stood as our float came by, and they all applauded...that made me feel better. As soon as it had passed, I headed back to our spot to see that we had not left any debris behind. Then I heard this motor scooter coming toward me asking for Jean Witte...What did I do now???? Well, he came to tell me we were needed at the reviewing stand because our float had won FIRST PRIZE!...it was a beautiful trophy, and a great end to a frustrating, yet adventure filled few weeks, and with a grateful heart also to Superintendent Al Banton, and all the others who pulled together to make this one of the most unexpected and happy days in my life.

Vikki came home from the hospital that afternoon and I took a nap...with pleasant dreams!

I have one more interesting story to tell about our first year with the Dale Fall Festival and Dr. Barrow...remember...he was the one who sat me down on a cold metal chair and had me hold the pan while he cut out my tonsils! He really was a neat guy a man, and his wife Estelle and I decided since his passion was delivering babies, we would contact as many of them as possible and get them into the parade. The success we had was fantastic. Since we live very close to Holiday World...it was called Santa Claus Land at the time of this event. I asked if we could borrow the little wooden train they had that had several seats and could hold all the people who had responded to our plea. And Dr. Barrow borrowed a true Surrey with the Fringe on Top, and a beautiful black Arabian horse that belonged to a man in Jasper named Alvin Ruxer. Of course this beautiful Surrey and horse merited a tuxedo and top hat, which the good doctor wore proudly. But we were not quite finished with his celebration...not just yet. Since I was on the steering committee for the parade, I set aside room for a booth which Mrs. Dr. Barrow

(Estelle) and I outfitted with a stork borrowed from The Baby Shop in Evansville, as well as a photo album filled with pictures of the 'babies' Dr. Barrow had delivered, and a note book in which the 'babies' as well as other well- wishers could write. It was among my greatest pleasures.

While I am on the subject of the Dale Fall Festival, I think you would enjoy knowing about my little town of Dale, Indiana. After having moved a bit in the previous years, Dale became my home...the place I met my husband and built the rest of my life.

Dale was a small town. About 600 people lived here when I first came in 1949, all the way up to approximately 2000 as of this writing. It was founded in 1846 and went by the name of Elizabeth. After someone realized there was another Elizabeth, IN, the name was changed to Dale. Interestingly, the feed mill that eventually ended up with my husband's family in 1930 was built in 1847 and owned by the Wallace family. Upon my arrival in Dale, I immediately felt warmth and a desire to stay...and I did!! In 1949 I counted all the businesses, one would find and for the 600ish people, we had these approximations: 1 bank, 1 post office, 1 medical doctor, 1 left handed dentist, 3 gas stations, 1 restaurant, 1 store that carried lumber and supplies for building, 1 furniture store, 1 'what-ever-you-might-want' store, 1 appliance store, 1 fabric and sewing store, 1 drug store, 4 grocery stores, 1 funeral home, with ambulance service, 2 barber shops, 4 taverns and 5 churches, and a few civic organizations. We also had a switchboard for our telephones and our phone number was 74W.

One story about how a switchboards telephone system worked in a small town concerned my in-laws-to-be who had gone to a movie one Sunday afternoon. The phone call came for them through the switchboard from their daughter who was in Chicago at the time. When the long distance operator from Chicago gave the switchboard operator the message as to who was calling and to whom they wished to speak, the operator promptly told the Chicago operator that the call could not be put through at that time because the people her party was wishing to speak to were at the movies and would be home later that evening. Does this remind you a bit about watching The Andy

Griffith Show when Andy calls someone and talks to his operator Sarah?

Leif Eskridge

Now I can't forget to tell about our garbage service. At this time there was no setting out of the trash cans for the big trucks to come by once a week to pick up and haul off to a big dump, and we had no sewage system in Dale except for the septic tanks which were buried in the ground and once in a while they even had to be cleaned out, lest they overflow and one was left to wonder why the grass was so much greener in a certain spot in the yard. Yes, indeed, we did have a unique garbage service.

There was an elderly man who had a horse and wagon and for a very small fee he would come to your house with his 'equipment' and haul your garbage away to never-never land! The man's name was Leif Eskridge, and our older daughter, Vikki, took a special liking to him and his garbage hauling set up and when he came to our house, she would get up into the wagon and sit beside Mr. Eskridge and ride over town in his wagon, as he made his collections. Vikki's first trip with

Mr. Eskridge was unbeknownst to us, so after searching frantically for her around our home, and not finding her, I finally got on the phone and found her at a friend's house, happy as a little bug, as though she were riding in a magnificent coach. It really doesn't take much to make people happy!!

Our community even came with a few, who, if you will pardon my being blunt, but were, as we said back then, not playing with a full deck. But this story also includes how our country *lived* 'inclusion' before it became a national movement.

Let's look back into the 1950's a bit. I was thinking about this the other day and decided there were some great moments to be recorded, as well as some very interesting facts. I don't remember when the nation made the startling discovery of 'inclusion', but it seems that all of a sudden there was a mad rush to be thoughtful and caring, and that in doing so we should include everyone...the era called 'inclusion'! But inclusion didn't start in the late 1980's or 90's! NO! Up until that time we had been living it on a daily basis and never giving it a second thought. We lived, worked and attended school with the slow learners, those who may be handicapped, and even those who, if you pardon my plain English, were just a bit off!

They were not shunned or criticized, they were a part of who we all were. I remember a sister of a friend of mine who was so crippled from polio that she went to school on crutches until technology gave her a motorized cart for her to get about on. When she needed help, there was always someone there to help her. There were two girls I especially remember when I was in high school, and I graduated high school in 1950, but one had a hip injury and needed assistance, and then there was the blind girl. I have always supposed that she must have been able to see enough to get something out of her school time, but she was there and she had help getting around.

Now the story I am about to tell is very real, and I do not intend to be abusive with my story, but just two doors down from where my husband and I raised our three children, lived a family that as was the saying back then: 'were not playing with a full deck'! They never really bothered anybody and they were never shunned by anyone. However;

I suppose the most colorful character in our neighborhood came from this family, and we all just watched his antics and helped him when need be. But I just have to relate some of what we dealt with on a daily basis.

This young man, now deceased, helped his brother work a beautiful vegetable garden and my family shared in this effort. The young man would often bring vegetables to our house and place them on a table on our screened porch. This was great! Then came clothing of differing kinds that appeared on my table, expecting me to mend them, and I did, also there were items that needed to be laundered, and I did. This young man's name was Talmadge and some days he would come up and just want to sit on the porch with me and talk. Of course his conversation was limited briefly to the weather.

Do any of you remember when people white-washed their trees? Well, Talmadge had two maple trees in his front yard which he kept white-washed. I honestly believe his motives were caring, especially when he brought his white-wash filled bucket to our house and told me he was going to white-wash our trees. However, the only trees we had at the time were a couple of fruit trees in our back yard. I thanked him kindly and without a word of disagreement, or discouragement, he took his white-wash bucket back home without painting our fruit trees. By the way, does any of the readers know what comprised the white-wash?

Then one day he decided he would help us out by mowing our lawn. We laughed so hard because the best way I can describe it is that it was done in a figure eight...so my husband straightened it out. Our Town Marshall often escorted this young man home whenever he appeared in public only partially dressed. I witnessed one such event one day when I looked out my kitchen window and this is what I saw: Talmadge was evidently ready for a fishing trip, and this is how he was dressed: He had on a hat, rubber boots, carried a bucket, a fishing pole over one shoulder, a shirt, but no pants...only underwear!! It was a laughable moment, but at the same time, one could see his weakness, and feel compassion. Talmadge died at the relatively young age of early forty's in an Indiana State hospital, and he was greatly missed.

I feel certain that by now you have begun to see what a variety of people we have in such a small spot in Indiana. Indeed, we were not short of the unusual! For instance, while our family doctor was from Dale, but practiced his medical profession in Huntingburg, IN., about 8 miles up the road from Dale,his mother, Flora and brother Bill lived in Dale. Our doctor's name was Fielding Williams, but it is his brother Bill I want to tell you about first.

Bill loved horses, but one could hardly believe he would still ride after having been thrown from a horse a few years earlier, rendering him so crippled that he could no longer walk, but the accident did not deter his enthusiasm for horses. He would ride to our house sometimes, and while his body movements were so crude and wavering, one could hardly believe he was able to stay on the horse, yet he did not hesitate to reach down and lift one of our children up onto the horse with him and take the child for a ride around town. Oh! Yes!, I was more than a bit concerned; however, I never doubted Bill's ability to bring my child back safely, even though with his laughter and the way his body went through contortions, you would swear he would surely fall from his horse. But it never happened.

Back in those days, I was having some medical problems and went to the hospital in Huntingburg several times. On one of those occasions, Bill was a patient there also. Since he knew me and my family quite well, he made visits to my hospital room in his wheel chair. In spite of the contortions of his body, and realizing he would be that way the rest of his life, Bill still have a wonderful sense of humor. I remember a few occasions while we were both recuperating, he would wheel himself into my hospital room with a funny story to tell. My surgical stitches prevented me from getting too happy...but not Bill. He would enter the room with a smile and his body enjoying his yet to be told story, to a point I told him he should stop the story telling because when he laughed, his poor body was going to laugh him right out of his chair. But he was somehow in control and that never happened...What a guy...what an attitude toward life, and what a wonderful, never-to-be-forgotten friend.

His brother, Dr. Fielding Williams, also a family friend, was one of the 'old tyme' doctor's...he even made house calls. I remember one night I was having one of my medical attacks that we were not sure just what to do about, and I had been sick enough that my husband and one year old daughter temporarily moved in with my in-laws. I was sleeping in a dimly lit room to myself, when I awoke around 4 am. I was in pain and I looked to the corner of this dimly lit bedroom, and whom did I see but Dr. Fielding Williams. Even in my pain, I was shocked to see him and asked what on earth he was doing in my bedroom at that time of morning. His reply: "I'm just looking after one of my patients." One more little bit of truth that our little town was never short of loving, caring people. Bill and Dr. Fielding Williams will never be forgotten.

I told these stories to remind people that when something seems so new and innovative…maybe it isn't. Like I said at the beginning of these stories, in the early years before we had so many government decrees, life was simple, uncomplicated and all inclusive!

So we had all that we needed, except maybe for a hospital, which was only 8 miles away. This was our own little slice of heaven, where the children played freely. In the summer time they would be out somewhere doing something from shortly after breakfast and with their chores done, only to return home for lunch, then out again until suppertime. After dark it was time to watch the stars, find the constellations and maybe catch lightening bugs! Or see a shooting star!! And we never locked the doors to our houses at night.

As for hometown entertainment, there were free movies in the city park, and once a year the Kiwanis Club sponsored a 'galloping Euchre party'. There were about 12 people in each participating home, filling three card tables. These were so much fun and always looked forward to. It seemed the entire community participated, and when the players had arrived at the home to which they were travelling, everything was so quiet. But when time was up and folks were ready to travel to their next destination, it sounded like the town had been invaded by giant mosquitoes'. There were other smaller games that were done by different groups and their preferences, but you couldn't beat the galloping euchre parties!

As time progressed, bowling leagues became very popular, and, along with a couple of bridge clubs and other card clubs, a 'Literary Club' was formed. And I must tell you that this group made sure anyone invited to join MUST know how to read. I feel I must tell this story because it hits very close to home! There was a vacancy in the Literary Club one year, and the group decided to invite my husband's aunt. Her last name was 'Witte' a much respected name in the community. Much to the embarrassment of the literary committee, Aunt Eliza was illiterate. Several years later, after I married into the Witte family, this same literary committee found themselves in a similar situation as with Eliza Witte. I was asked to join, and after I passed the literary test and was accepted in the club, I was told of the literary goof-up some years before.

It should come as no surprise that along with the many varied people, places, occupations and whatever, there are a multitude of stories and I would like to share as many of those as I can remember. Because all I am writing about is factual! We lived it in Dale, and I lived my life from 1932 until today in various places! What a wonderful life I have been given!

Aside from the variety of stores our little town boasted, the people who ran the stores and lived in the community is where the depth of life really came. Having told of Mr. Eskridge and his garbage 'wagon', and the slip up of the Literary Club, I will give you probably more information about the people and places than you really care to know. I have even told you a bit about one of the greatest Fall Festival's in the Mid-West, which is still taking place each year, the week-end after Labor Day, having started in 1968. At the present writing it is 2019. What a fantastic record and I am pleased and honored to have been chosen to serve on the steering committee. The weekend following Labor Day was chosen because the festival had to use the benches from Lincoln State Park, which closed on Labor Day. All things work for good to those who love the Lord!!

The festival itself had many interesting events. Amazingly, it seemed there were certain people who were, as one might say, 'just made to fit their job'. Of course, the banker was the one who took care of making all the deposits of money that was made from the different events. There were many food stands. After all isn't that what people like to do most...eat?? There were elephant ears, managed by the St. Joseph

Catholic Church. So they had no problem finding people to serve their turns. The polish sausage along with hot dogs, kraut, sautéed green peppers and onions…Yum! A stand that is run faithfully by Malee Burress! There was also offered turtle soup, caramel apples, ice cream and candy taffy if you wanted something special. If you wanted a full meal we offered thick grilled pork chops, fried chicken, potato salad, baked beans and slaw. Another of our specialties went to our hamburger stand. This was soon named Gus Burger. So named for the man who put the stand together, grilled hamburgers with a taste one could get no place else. His name was Gus Wilzynski. This sweet man has passed on, but his 'Gus Burgers' still are served at every festival. There were drinks of varied kinds, and of course, every German community must have a beer garden. It was in the beer garden that music was played, usually country western. The beer garden was also a place where I was about as afraid as any time I can remember. Being on the steering committee also meant that I look out for things that shouldn't be happening and correct them if I could. I had witnessed some teen-agers, not only in the beer garden, but they were leaving with a stash hidden in their jackets. It was rather late I actually was headed home which was just across a couple of people's yards. I talked with the guy's running the beer garden, and even though I could see they were pretty good sized men, they suddenly became giants, when not complying with my suggestion that they stop what they were doing. Their response was something other than respectful…so I stepped behind the counter and pulled the electric plugs, and told the guy's that their job was finished for the night…and I headed for home, like I said…scared to death one of these giants was sure to follow me. Safe at last, home hadn't looked so good to me in a long time…WHEW!!

As a counterpart, there was a stage in front of the grounds where one could listen to good ole Southern Gospel music. It seemed we could always have a great crowd enjoying this good ole music!!

The first year of the Dale Fall Festival our innovative kids along with some help from some parents, built a "Root Beer Garden" float. It was really neat. On the bed of a farm wagon we shaped a giant root beer mug of chicken wire. Gail had some pipe he bent to make the handle.

We got a long handle from a janitor type broom, wrapped it in white paper and wound red ribbon around it to look like a straw. Then we took paper napkins and filled the holes in the chicken wire and sprayed most of it brown to look like real root beer, leaving enough of it white to look like foam running over the side of the mug. We polished the float off with a soda shop table and a couple of chairs, hooked the wagon to a pick-up truck and entered the parade. Then we put the wagon in the Root Beer Garden for the kids, to counter the real beer garden. The younger generation managed to have groups of their own genre to play music to their liking.

Of course there was a Queen pageant. This one was given to me to run, and I loved every minute of it. My team and I patterned it after the Miss Indiana pageant, and we had eight to ten beautiful and talented girls each year. From the Dale pageant, the winner got to participate in the Miss Freedom Festival, held in Evansville, IN. .....and if she won there, she could be eligible to enter the Miss Indiana pageant. It turned out to be quite good in helping develop these young girls, and it also is still going, although I long ago retired from that position.

We also had pageants for the younger kids, boys and girls. There was a contest to see whose baby could crawl the farthest, whose baby was the cutest, a basketball contest, a raffle with some really nice prizes, a cake walk, bingo, carnival rides, hog wrestling, my great granddaughters participated in that. The fire department was there to hose down the mud from these fantastic kids. There were barbeque and steak cooking contests, and a good time was had by all...even those who willingly helped clean up so early Sunday morning that by the time most people got up, one would wonder if the weekend had only been a dream. One contest that my great granddaughters Katie and Kyla enter each year is the hog wrestling. They wrestled in teams of four. If you can imagine mostly girls entering this contest ready to jump into a pit of mud along with an already muddy hog and try to grab that slick hog and put this fella on a center platform. The team who accomplishes this in the least amount of time is declared the winner. Then, here comes the fire department to hose down and remove as much of the mud from these participants as possible!

When you have a quaint community with a variety of stores, churches, etc., it can only follow that there will be people of different varieties and personalities. I feel certain you will find some interesting ones, and some even are sad stories that I feel necessary in order to understand some of the good, the bad and the ugly!! Some people even had memorable nicknames: Dumpy Walters was a neighbor and fisherman, 'Poot' Thorpe, a rather nondescript man and 'Pug' Nord. Now 'Pug' had one memorable moment. It happened when he was in high school and Gail's Aunt Sadie was the Home Economics teacher who was never afraid to correct a wrong. One day Pug was walking rather nonchalantly down a school hallway and decided to pull the string outing one of the hallway lights. Just so happened Aunt Sadie was right behind him. Now this was not a serious offense, but back then most teachers had a very authoritative voice, and jurisdiction, and Aunt Sadie asked Pug why he felt it necessary to turn the light out. Pug very innocently said: "Because I felt like it." WRONG ANSWER!! Aunt Sadie, in her sternest teacher authoritative voice said: "Young man, just how long have you been running this school?" When a teacher speaks to you in *that* voice you had better have a good reply, and Pug's was: …."aaaahhh, about 15 minutes!" and immediately removed himself from the presence of Aunt Sadie and her teacher voice! No punishment, but it was a memorable enough moment that the town has remembered this all these many years. *I think Aunt Sadie surely giggled a bit after 'Pug' left her sight!!*

While we are at school, I can tell another incident that happened years later when my kids were in school. We had a nice man teaching French, named Ken Murphy, who drove a neat little Volkswagen. And no one should have anything against him. But when you are boys in high school, just like Pug, you don't really need a reason for what you do. So even though there were no qualms with Mr. Murphy, in preparing to leave for school one day, he could not find his car. I don't know if he notified the authorities or not, but he walked to school, only to find his vehicle sitting on the stage in the auditorium of the school. Now why on earth would anyone do something like that?? Well, they were high school teenagers having fun with a teacher. No other explanation needed. This same group of boys found it necessary to totally dismantle another students bicycle one day...not a good idea!!! This time we had a 'no nonsense' principal, Mr. Kifer, who found out who the boys were, called them into his office and had the owner of the bicycle get a cost to repair his bike and Mr. Kifer divided the cost among the 5 boys (one of which was my son, Rick) and they had to pay for their mistake! Good lesson!!

I was very much involved in school activities, serving on committees of all sorts or chaperoning groups to whatever competition was coming up. At this time in history, the floors of basketball courts, especially in Indiana where basketball is king, were hallowed grounds. The kids needed a place to release some of their energy and/or frustrations following a ball game, and I thought it would be nice to dance in the gym, but when I met with the powers that be, I was told that no street shoes were allowed. I asked if the removal of shoes and dancing in sock feet would work. YES!! I felt like we were getting ready to embark on a new frontier. But we needed some rules...sooo...I met with the guidance counselor, Mr. Etienne, who was on board with the idea and said we should meet with the student council and together we set up the guidelines. They were simple, and we were ready for fun. Mostly the kids danced to records. Since a fee of 50 cents was charged to attend the dance, when we had enough money in the coffers, we would hire a real live band. Real fun!

One interesting incident I encountered occurred in the spring when kids loved water pistols. I had already heard that the school was having some difficulty in keeping the water pistols out of the class rooms. Interesting to note the difference in the 1960's, 70' and even 80's there were no real threats with real guns such as we have all too often in many schools today! What a wonderful era this was, and I am so glad my children were able to realize it.

Dance night came along with the water pistol issue and I devised a plan that I was sure would take care of it. However, when the dance was about to begin, I noticed one teacher, Mr. Rosbottom and the principal, Mr. Tislow standing off to the side watching me. I asked if they had decided to attend the dance. They said they had only come to watch me as I experienced my problems with the water pistols. I just walked over to them and told them one had to smarter than the kids. They were eager to see my plan of action, so I brought out a plastic bucket, and told them that as each student came in I asked that they deposit their 'weapon' in the bucket. I took down their name and told them that at the end of the dance they would get their water pistol back; however, should I find one in the possession of any student in the gym, they would immediately be removed from the gym. I had absolutely no problem with the students, but left two school officials with a bit of egg on their faces. That really felt kinda good!!!

We had another school teacher with whom I worked out a neat plan. His name was Charles 'Chuck' Manchester. He was the band teacher. This was about the time our son, Rick was too young to yet play in the band, but he had a definite ear for music and since our piano was in the living room along with our TV, Rick soon started playing the theme songs from many of the shows. Since Mr. Manchester taught music, I approached him about giving our son some piano lessons. He told me his piano teaching ability was very limited but he was willing to give it a try, especially when I asked him, being a bachelor, if he would accept as payment for the lesson a home cooked meal? I found that his favorite meal was pancakes and sausage. Our Monday night meal became pancakes and sausage for about a year. That was a pretty good deal, don't you think?

Along with being the proud mother of the most wonderful son, came also a sticky situation when one night as Gail and I returned from bowling and found our cherubs asleep, I noticed a paper on the kitchen table with this message: "Due to lack of interest tomorrow has been cancelled." I immediately noticed with a bit of pride, the unique way Rick had of leaving us a message. Come morning, I hit the phones, calling friends telling them the kids didn't have school that day for some unknown reason. About 7:30 Rick comes bounding down the stairs a bit unhappy because he was late getting ready for school. Of course, I reminded him of the little note he had left for me the night before. Imagine his shock! "No, Mom, school hasn't been called off, that was just something I saw on the board that I thought was kinda neat!"

Imagine the scurrying I did to call all the mothers I had just given the 'stay-at-home' message that I was wrong!! Oh, boy! I was sure I would be in trouble with the principal, so I called and told him the situation. He only laughed and told me he was wondering why half of the freshman class was missing! WHEW!! Another hair-raising moment of motherhood that ended all right!

When our local Girl Scout troop was planning a few nights in the woods, our brave leader, Jane Davis, asked me to come along. In true Girl Scout manner, we cooked our supper over an open fire, and then used the remains of the fire for dessert...roasted marshmallows, some of which became 's'mores'. It was a hot summer night and someone got the hose out, not only to put out our fire, but to cool us off before bedtime. Let me tell you...when you go to bed in the woods you are in the *dark!!* At least we had permanent tent set-up's. We had twelve Girl Scouts and four girls were assigned to each of three tents, while Jane and I were treated to our own 2-man tent.

Time for sleep, which should come easily as there was not even a sliver of a moon...*NOT a sliver!* Just as Jane and I were about to dose off, tent #3 let out a war hoop!! What on earth could be happening? Tent #3 was soon joined by tent's number 1 and 2 rousing Jane and me from the story telling we were doing in our tent to help us go to sleep. We jumped and ran to what we figured had to be a tragedy. We found the girls from tent #3 sitting in tent 2 and crying and screaming and soon joined by tent 1. So the screaming got louder and more frantic. *What on earth?* Jane pleaded with the girls to please find someone who can speak coherently and let us know what happened!! All we heard was: "*A spider!!!* Oh! Just a spider? Well it wasn't just any old spider. We soon found that it was a wolf spider! I soon found out that everyone knew what a wolf spider was but me. After we got back home I did a bit of research to satisfy my curiosity, and it seems they are pretty big, but my ignorance of spiders showed itself again when I read that they could be as large as 30 milometers...I only deal in inches, and pounds and the likes, so I still didn't know how big our new found 'friend' was, but I did note that it was big enough to scare the living daylights out of 12 Girl Scouts, and that was enough for me!! Our present problem was:

What can we do to stop the screaming, so we just decided to join them and have a 'scream-along'!! It worked, because the girls thought it a bit funny to have their leaders screaming too, and they started laughing at us…problem partially solved. We had intended to spend two nights, but nixed that, lest we have another night visitor.

So it was up early, after a much shorter night's sleep than we would have liked, and good ole Girl Scout breakfast over the fire. Jane decided to make sure we did all that we could under the circumstances we would take a short hike in the woods, pack up and go home. The hike was just long enough for 3 of the girls to get a good dose of poison ivy. Oh! My! Aren't these camp outs great? Well, at least this one was especially memorable.

In January 1973, Sarah entered the brand new high school in Lincoln City, IN, a product of consolidation. The name for the new school was chosen appropriately as Heritage Hills, referring to the rich heritage in our community of Abraham Lincoln. With Rick away at school at IU, he felt that the new school should have a new school song, rather than one as patterned so often from colleges. So he penned the melody and waited eagerly to return home and contact the two band directors so, as were his words,:…"I could hear what it sounds like."

With the help of the band directors the woodwinds and percussions were added and it was accepted by the school board as the official school song of Heritage Hills High School. Two years later Rick was invited to attend one of the football games and given the privilege of directing the Heritage Hills High School band with *his* gift to the community he had grown up in. What a proud night for Mom and Dad also!

I mentioned that Hoosier basketball is king, I would like to tell you a bit about some real standouts that will show you that you do not have to come from a big city to make your mark in the world. This world I speak of is *basketball!!* This story goes back into the late 1950's and the community of Dale was treated to four years of some of the best basketball I can remember. Every Friday night most of Dale gathered in the Dale gym or would travel to see games played on the road, as Roger Kaiser and buddy Bob Reinhart put on a virtual basketball clinic. Roger and Bob just worked together naturally, or maybe it is because of their love for the sport, they cut their teeth on the game. Roger told me that he and buddy Bob were shooting hoops from the time they were third graders. It showed in the way that they played the game. Roger developed a two hand jump shot that was a sight to behold. When he had the ball and took the jump we knew we had two points. But Roger didn't stop when he graduated Dale High School. One would think a star like this would be bound for Indiana University, but Roger took a different trail and went to Georgia Tech. In my conversation with him recently, he told me he wasn't sold on staying at Tech, but when the coach looks at you and says 'Georgia Tech needs you!' that could make a difference, and it did. Roger was All American two years in a row and has about as much jewelry as a retail store, as well as trophies and other accolades. He coached for over 50 years. Roger is now comfortably retired and living in Carrollton, Ga with his wife Beverly, who was his high school sweetheart and, as Roger said she is the backbone of his life. My son-in-law Kenny Neighbors, who is a great golfer, has had the pleasure many times of playing golf at Christmas Lake golf course and others in the area with both Roger and Del Harris...maybe Bob Reinhart also. Just a great group of gentlemen! And I feel so honored to know them also. I am thankful for their contribution to making a name for themselves starting in little ole Dale, IN.

Dale played host to another 'to-be celebrity'. Del Harris's name is not new to the world of basketball either, and Dale, Indiana had the chance to see him coach our high school team for 2 years, in 1962-'63 and 1963-'64 seasons. He left Dale to coach at Spencer, IN, and Earlham College, and possibly others before he coached some professional teams, among which were the Houston Rockets, the Milwaukee Bucks', and Golden State Warriors. In my conversation with him the other day, I found that he and Roger have both given up coaching after 40 or 50+ years. Del says he is working in front offices now and enjoying his life in Frisco, Texas. Del was not only a great basketball coach, he is also an ordained minister. I'm sure there are many games he has felt the need to pray for! I remember him as just a real nice guy. Even though he lives in Texas, by the time he got finished listing the multitude of relatives he has around Dale, I felt he was related to everyone but me...I'm an import. The only relatives I have around Dale are ones my husband and I have, and I am proud of most all of them!!

Music was a mainstay not only within our family, but it permeated throughout our community and spread to other communities with one thing in common…we loved to sing! A group of rag-tag singers, who actually had marvelous voices, and a group called The Bel-Canto Singers was formed. There was a young man whom God had blessed with a remarkable talent, not only for playing music, but directing it. His name was John Schum. It was he who named the group. He was organist for St. Joseph Catholic Church in Dale, and had close contact with the Benedictine nuns who were in Ferdinand, IN about 5 miles from Dale. So John recruited several of the nuns to sing, and one who was just what we needed on the piano. The people who comprised this group were not only the nuns, but school teachers, business men and women, housewives and students. Shortly after organizing, we made an album…one of those plastic thingy's that played at 33 RPM's (what did that stand for?) The name of the album was "No Greater Love" a beautiful piece by John Peterson. After a few seasons of singing in different churches, the group sort of drifted apart. Then one evening John Schum came to my house and asked if I thought we could breathe some life back into the Bel- Canto's. I told him I would try, and wrote down as many names as I could remember, and never once got a declining answer. We just LOVED to SING!! There were many glorious nights of rehearsal and finally we presented out final concert at St Mary's Catholic Church in Huntingburg, IN, where we brought the house to its feet and tears to many eyes as we absolutely did composer Handel proud with our rendition of "The Hallelujah Chorus"…what a moment…what an exit! The Bel Canto's retired for good after that, and not but a couple of years afterwards, our beloved director passed away.

I mentioned that our town had several businesses, and one of them was the appliance store run by Dwight Springston. Dwight may have known a lot about appliances, but it would take an appliance scholar to understand what he told about them. He used technical names, where most of us just spoke plain English. But he was a very nice man and willing to help whenever someone needed him. Sad to say, his life ended in drowning in the lake the town built just outside the town limits, and appropriately named 'Dale Lake'. The lake held some pretty good fish, so I am told, and played host to many a family picnic, but also laid claim to two other town members. In addition to Dwight's death, the Methodist minister and the local dentist, Dr. Brown also drowned in our lake. All three men were avid fishermen but evidently not great swimmers. We had a hard time dealing with their untimely deaths.

Dr. Brown was our dentist...the only left-handed dentist I have ever known. He had his office in a room in his home in downtown Dale where he lived with his wife Edna and two daughters, Gloria and Priscilla. The Methodist minister was relatively new to Dale, and I did not know much about him. But he had been one of ours and we missed him, too.

Our town was not lacking in adventure, be it good or bad, and I have another both bad, and sad story. It concerns a married couple and a couple of men with a vengeance. It seems there was some concern over the custody of a child and, as the story was told to me, the grandfather of the child got word that the mother of the child would be at a certain place at a certain time. It was Christmas time, and things were not so merry, because the grandfather had been ready to take the life of the mother and stop the battle of the custody of this child. Life has many twists and turns, and this was a terrible one, since there was an innocent lady at this place where the mother of the child was supposed to be. The innocent one went to the shop to purchase a gun for her husband for Christmas, only to be dealt a terrible blow from the child's grandfather's gun, which took her life...**wrong woman...!!!** At least the guilty man was found guilty of first degree murder and spent the rest of this life in prison, while the fate of the child was left unresolved and the father, who had also been implicated as having encouraged his dad to commit this dastardly crime was left to live and never have to answer to any authorities for his encouragement, for which I guess there are no laws! Surely the father has had many a sleepless night.

Only recently I learned of the apparent murder/suicide of the father and his current wife. There seems to be an air of mystery still lingering. The child, who is now grown is married and lives in Hawaii. The child's mother…the intended victim, was our next door neighbor at the time. She told me that indeed she was supposed to have been at the place of the murder, but her duties as a nurse changed her plan, and ultimately saved her life, and caused an unanswerable and horrible mistake! A part of the ugly!!

Speaking of ugly, I have one more 'ugly' and no more!! Soon after our first child was born and I had been through a couple of major surgeries, Gail hired a lady to help me with some of the house work. One day a couple of my friends came by for lunch. Well, actually they were more than just friends, they were relatives. I had planned lunch for _all_ of us. Our hired lady, Virginia, was from one of only two black families we had around Dale, but she always had lunch with us. She fit well in our environment. Our unpleasant surprise came when the table was set for lunch and the relatives refused to be seated at the same table with Virginia. Of course, Virginia graciously left the room. I followed her and apologized profusely, but the damage was done. And now, looking back on the situation, I only wish my husband and I had had the gumption to just excuse lunch altogether, or something. Sadly we didn't and I sincerely hope there is never such an incident in our household again! Just another UGLY!!

As life progresses, families grow, and I have told you already about Rick and Regina's family, and Vikki's son Jonathan, so now I can move to Sarah's family and tell more. You already know of Elana and her beauty, but I have a few more about Elana. Now Elana was no real athlete, but her mother thought she should play some sort of sport, so she was introduced to soccer. At one of the soccer matches we couldn't find Elana in the spot she should be, but it didn't take long until we spotted her, sitting off the side of the soccer field picking flowers. That is when we knew she was better off in beauty pageants.

Elana started in beauty pageants at age two. We entered her in a pageant in Lexington, KY. First of all she entertained our dinner table by eating lemon wedges. Of course there were not many of us who could unlock our jaws to carry on a conversation. It was unreal! She loved them! But she came off as no sour lemon at the pageant where she won most photogenic. This was just the beginning of the many trips Sarah and I would make to find her the proper dress and then let her be 'Elana'! Every pageant she entered she came home with a trophy. At age four in a pageant in Louisville, KY, she came in second and also won 'overall most beautiful'. We heard of a school in Nashville, TN in which the lady owner, Miss Marie, was prepping young girls the proper techniques of pageantry. Miss Marie also was interested in helping develop talent and she organized a group called "Kids Can Sing Too". Of course Elana wanted to participate and for a couple of years, every Saturday, Sarah and I made the trek from Santa Claus, IN to Nashville. Extra trips were made to see the performances of these talented youngsters.

While in Nashville, we heard of a beauty pageant called "Dixie Darling". Again we entered Elana. I was working for H&R Block at this time and was unable to attend, and this time Elana returned with a trophy almost as tall as she at age five and with the title of "Miss Dixie Darling". Somewhere along the line these pageants stopped, but Elana didn't. While she attended Heritage Hills High School, she won parts in all of the musicals. And even had a part, both singing and dancing in "Crazy for You" and "Kiss Me Kate". Her final achievement in beauty pageants was in 2003 when she won Miss Spencer County. It was at this pageant that she met the man she would marry. Now she judges beauty pageants and after receiving training in the art of applying make-up, she also is often called on to tend to the make-up of a pageant hopeful or a soon-to-be bride, filling the rest of her time as a stay at home mom, loving mother and wife.

In 2004 she married one of the nicest young men, Justin Epple, the one she met at the Spencer County pageant, and they now live in Evansville with their two daughters Katie and Kyla. Kyla, of course is the reason I started this story...remember...Kyla didn't know what a telephone was, and it sparked my interest in backing up many years and drawing from my own experiences as a youngster growing up.

Elana and Justin are leaders in our church and have a wonderful family relationship with the Lord. I feel so blessed.

A 'thing' with kids has always been...'tell me a story about mommy or daddy when they were little.' So here I go spilling the beans on Elana.

I have already told you of her un-athletic ability. But I have a couple more I'm sure she won't mind my sharing with you.

When she was only about 6 months old her mother and I took her to Florida to visit family and friends, but Elana got sick. And one day while Sarah was visiting a friend I noticed Elana had a fever, and I became quite concerned, but didn't have a way of contacting Sarah, and she had my car. So I rocked and sang to my feverish first grandchild, becoming more concerned by the minute. I didn't really know what to sing to her so I made up my own song which went something like this: "Bye, oh little baby"…at this point I couldn't find a word to say next, because I was singing to her and her name is Elana Marie…so I completed my little tune thus…"Bye, oh 'Lana-Rie, Bye oh little baby, sweet as she can be…bye oh little baby, bye oh 'Lana-rie". It made a soothing song, she slept and the nick-name 'Lana-Rie' still is with her today. Just to let you know, her mom came back soon and we took 'Lana-Rie' to a pediatrician and got medication and she was well in no time!

She also knew that I loved her more than life itself and would never, ever spank her. But one day at my house, I caught her into something she shouldn't be into…harmless as it was, I felt I should discipline. But how could I when this sweet little four or five year old girl looked up at me and said, mournfully: "Oh! Mema, you're not going to spank your little 'Lana-Rie?" Case closed!!

Talk about being scared?? One day when Kenny and Sarah were living on Medcalf Street in Dale, Four year old Elana was playing in the front yard when a neighbor came running to Sarah, so scared she was shaking. This is what she told happened from her point of view on her front porch: Elana stepped out into the highway at the same time a semi-truck came by, and according to her eye witness, the truck ran over Elana…or rather seemingly ran through her. As the report continued, she saw the child run through by the semi; yet Elana walked back into the yard, and the truck continued on its way as though nothing happened. I would not have put this story in here unless I felt confident of what the neighbor saw. Was it one of those miracles, where it was just not Elana's time to die? We are all thankful for that!!

But then there was another time when we were coming back from a trip to Evansville, and while in the car I had the radio playing of Garrison Keillor singing "Will you love me when I'm old?" I nonchalantly reached over and patted my sweet lil 'Lana-Rie on the knee and asked her: "Will you love ME when I'm old?" By this time in her life she had reached the age of looking at everyone 15 years older than her as being old. So her 'loving' response to my question was...are you ready for this??? *"Mema, you are old."* I threatened to stop the car and leave her bedside the road...but I didn't!!

As the years have passed, she has become such a help to me along with her two girls since I moved to Evansville. And her husband was a keeper the first time she brought him into our home. Again, I count my blessings, and they keep getting taller and taller!

Then Kenny and Sarah had Jade. What a strong-willed child! lol She popped out of the womb with an attitude. Her childhood was sort of hard because of her unmovable strong will, but as she matured that strong will was tempered with loyalty and dependability and blossomed into a beautiful young woman. And this one was the athlete of the family! Her dad had come from a family of athletic boys and he gladly settled for an athletic daughter. Being 6' tall she took her athletic ability to the volleyball court where she played high school and KIVA (Kentucky Indiana Volleyball Association) based in Louisville, which gave her the opportunity to travel across America using her skill. I was fortunate enough to attend most of her practices and many of her games across the country. She went with her KIVA team to Russia and even received a full ride scholarship to play with the Mobile, Alabama Jaguars. But due to a recurring problem with her back, She chose to give up her scholarship and come back to Indiana and finished her college at Indiana State University, in Terre Haute. She met a young man, Adam Hooper and together they have 2 of my great blessings...Aiden who is 6 and his sister, Kendall, who is her mother made over and will be 4 in September. The first marriage didn't work out, so after the break- up, She persevered. She is now happily remarried to Trey Russell, soon to be Dr. Trey Russell the chiropractor, and is living in Atlanta and here are some of her accomplishments.

Having combined all the skills necessary for success in today's world, along with her strong will and wonderful work ethic, Jade achieved honors as a student at Indiana State University, Terre Haute, and has endeared herself in the 'hospitality' world of business by applying skills leaned in university to build the success of multiple wood cabinetry brands while employed at Masterbrand at Jasper, where she soon became senior product and market analyst. A year or so later, she was hired by Kimball International, also of Jasper. Still advancing, she applied her talents and skills with Decolav International and became senior director of new business development throughout the US and Canada. In essence, her job is to make sure you are able to enjoy the comfort, beauty and full hospitality area of any of the hotels her company services, both in the US an in other countries of the world. WOW!!! Now, still living in Atlanta, she is continuing to grow and develop and she watches her children grow and her husband become a doctor. She is a wonderful wife and mother and I believe she can accomplish anything she sets her mind to…she is my granddaughter and I am so proud of her as I am her sisters who have each chosen different paths. I am so blessed!

Daughter #3 in the Neighbors household was Autumn. This little girl had a combination of the laid back style of Elana, As well as the athletic ability of Jade. But as Autumn achieved adulthood, her heart turned to teaching and missions. But while she was still quite young, she spent quite a bit of time at my house or at the Mill with her dad. Sarah was selling insurance at this time and her hours varied and I enjoyed the time I had with her. Interestingly, one of her favorite pastimes at my house was rummaging through my waste paper baskets. I don't think even she knew quite what, if anything in particular she was looking for. It just seemed to be fun for her and it certainly did no harm.

One day when Sarah was not working, she came to visit me along with Autumn. As Sarah and I were deep into conversation, we realized we had not seen nor heard anything from Autumn for a bit, so we decided to check it out. After exhausting virtually every idea, we almost began to panic when I decided to check upstairs. She was about 4 years old but evidently got tired and decided to take a nap. Since I still kept a baby crib upstairs we were a bit surprised and relieved to find that she had climbed the stairs, climbed into the crib, covered herself with a quilt and was sound asleep. I told you she was laid back, but I didn't know kids would actually do anything like that. Where was she when my own were growing up??

Since Autumn was a frequent visitor, we had a very good and loving relationship. But if anyone were to have come into my house at a time when she and I were playing cards, you would have had a different view of that relationship. I have no idea how or when this started, but we would call each other names such as 'cheater', or maybe even 'you are the most idiotic card player I have ever known.' And it escalated from there while enjoying every dig we could dish out, and we could both take and receive! Just an unusual memory that neither of us will ever forget! And on my birthday last year, Autumn gave me a card that reminded me of those fun filled days with our card games. The card read: " Whatever Happens at Grandma's Stays at Grandma's." She knew I would understand!!

Should she happen to be in the company of her dad, whom she always proudly referred to as her 'best bud', she still liked her naptime. Kenny often cleaned soybeans or wheat for his customers and if it came Autumn's naptime, she would find a stack of feed sacks and 'sack out' for a while.

Autumn was also pretty good at sports and played volleyball while in high school, but her heart was in teaching and in mission work. While still in high school, she did her student teaching at David Turnham Elementary which I could see from my kitchen window in our home in Dale. It was not unusual for me to receive a phone call as she prepared to leave one school for the other and place an order for me to have a PB&J (peanut butter and jelly sandwich) ready for her as she went from her learning classroom to her teaching class room.

After graduating high school Autumn studied at Indiana Weslyan College with a double major in Elementary Education and Exceptional Needs, K-6. Graduating from IWU in 2012, she couldn't wait to spread her wings so she went to Honduras where she taught for two years. She fell in love not only with the children she taught, but also with their families. It is my belief that if she could have made it happen, she would have brought a few of these lovable Gospel hungry Honduran children home with her.

When she returned to the United States she became an elementary teacher here in Evansville, IN and will finish her seventh year of teaching at Harper Elementary the end of school year 2019. In 2010 she met and married a wonderful young man with a burning heart such as hers for spreading the Gospel of Jesus Christ. Josh Murray is a perfect match for Autumn and she, husband Josh and baby Nolan plan to leave on January, 31st for an extended stay back in Honduras where she will have an administrative role at a children's home called Rancho Ebenezer. Josh will be working with counselors to support them in their devotions with the children at the ranch as well as teaching the children basis computer skills and knowledge, while Autumn will also be mentoring and training teachers, selecting and purchasing school curriculum and helping to keep the school unified between North American and Honduran staff. And all three of them will be studying Spanish as their second language. And precious little 16 month old Nolan is still wondering what in the world is going on!! They have committed to serving with World Gospel Outreach for 4 years, with the possibility of staying longer.

This summer I am trying to enjoy as much time as I can with Autumn and Josh and watch baby Nolan develop. He has such a sweet disposition and a ready smile. But at nine months, mom says he is also learning temper tantrums! Welcome to the world of child rearing!

The family they are leaving behind here in the states will miss them terribly, but they are doing what they feel the Lord is leading them to do and they will have a furlough each year. Little Nolan will have his first birthday September, 24th before they plan to leave on their adventure for the Lord in January, 2020! Prayers are always needed and appreciated when you undertake such a giant step in FAITH!

****

Our trip to Europe and a bit of a tribute to President Eisenhower

As yet I have not figured out how to adequately express to the world just how blest I have been through the good and bad the painful and happy. One does not have to live long to understand that into each life rain does have to fall, and one of the best parts of that is that following the rain is the beautiful rainbow of God's promise!

In 1974 Gail and I were asked to represent our business of dealing with animal feeds and grains (Agribusiness) on a three week trip to Europe as a part of the People to People organization. What an honor! People to People was a brain child of President Dwight Eisenhower. As a dealer in feed and grain, we, along with approximately twenty other people, mostly couples, were to visit a representative business in five different European countries. During the day we would visit a business and in the evening our group met with the counterparts we had been with during the day and have dinner. What a wonderful way it was to get to know these people from a business standpoint as well as a more relaxed evening learning more about these wonderful people as we soon found were much like us.. First we landed at Heathrow airport in London. England. Our first day was visiting the Stock Exchange and had the privilege of being the very first group where women were allowed in the balcony of the Exchange. We never knew if later women were allowed on the floor of the Exchange, but at least we had the honor of viewing from the balcony. Then we had lunch at an honest to goodness British Pub enjoying what else but fish and chips. In the evening, we had dinner at our host Hotel the Metropole. And another day while still in London we visited a mill where they manufactured flour, not too unlike what our business did in Indiana. We were also treated to watching the changing of the guard at Buckingham Palace. And boy! do the British love their desserts. No low fat deals here. They served only the good stuff and we were sure we didn't want to know the calorie count.

After about three days in London we boarded a train for Oslo, Norway. WOW! This was a bit different for Indiana. First with Norway being closer to the North Pole, during August daylight hardly went to sleep. It took a couple of nights before we could get used to Oslo being very much alive at three am...or are we just that old? The Fijords were something I had only read about in books, but we really did have a boat ride through some of them. Since nighttime was very short we had a problem finding time to sleep. And just outside our hotel the strangest thing happened after dinner. We called them the portable retail stores, because business minded people would bring their wares just outside the hotel and actually spread cloths on the sidewalks and then it was shop, shop, shop. We felt as though we were in the very heart of Oslo because just up the street from our hotel was the kings residence. Didn't see the king, but he had a very nice house. Two interesting things we learned about Norway was that they grow carrots in abundance, and as one of our guides told us… kids were born with skis on! We didn't quite buy that, but then we were not treated to any Norwegian births while visiting their beautiful country. While none of our group was awarded the Nobel Peace Prize, we at least visited the building where the deed was done, and we even sat at the table where the awards were given.

From Norway we went to Sweden. It was so neat to walk on the cobblestone streets in down-town Stockholm. Gail and I had just celebrated our 24th wedding anniversary on the 6th of August, and even though it was a year early for the silver anniversary, and a few weeks late for the actual anniversary, Stockholm helped us celebrate anyway… totally unexpectedly, we were presented with a bouquet of flowers and a hand painted Dalecarlian horse. We were told that this horse held a special meaning for newlyweds. It was to be hung over a doorway in the home as a symbol of their aspirations of owning a horse of their own for the farming that would be done. What a nice surprise, but they were not finished with us yet! When we got back to our hotel room, waiting for us was a bottle of champagne and glasses for sharing this special evening with some special friends.

After leaving Sweden we went to Warsaw, Poland. This was probably my favorite place. There was so much history and some of the warmest people we had ever met. Our tour guides name was Alexandria, and Gail wanted to bring her home with us, and I believe she would have gladly come with us if she could have. There were some of the lowest points and highest points of our trip. While we visited places bearing a strong reminder of the wars so many years ago, we were also treated to a most fascinating concert in a place called Chopin Park. Seating was built into the hillside and in the center of the park was a huge rock that created a natural stage for the concert. No microphones were used, just beautiful artistry wafting throughout the park…beautiful classical music that will forever stay in my mind.

Interestingly, there was very little crime! I mean they just didn't mess around. There were numerous vendors that surrounded an area within walking distance of our hotel and at night they simply lowered the awning on their carts and went home, not worrying about someone stealing their merchandise. And the people...oh, yes the people...we spoke no Polish and most spoke no English. Such was the case at dinner one evening as I was seated by our bus driver. Believe it or not, there was never a dull or awkward moment and by the time the evening was over we had overcome our language barrier and I knew a lot about the bus driver as well as his family. Pictures and facial expressions as well as gestures bridged the gap beautifully. Yes, Warsaw Poland was one of my very favorite places, and the eve of our departure for Vienna, Austria, we had dinner in a mansion that was owned by Jackie Kennedy's grandfather.

One other thing we found that the Polish people like is VODKA! And the waiter never let us see the bottom of our little vodka glass... and dessert!!...Ice cream inside a topaz crystal edible dish that you crack to enjoy the entire treat. (Pardon my ignorance if there is a special name for this dessert...I didn't bother to ask...just enjoyed.) It was also while in Sweden that we visited a capitalist dairy farmer...a bit unusual for Sweden, but here we were enjoying strawberry shortcake and the announcement came over the air waves that President Nixon had resigned his position...remember Watergate??

Next stop was Austria.

We were seeing more and more of the love for classical music and in Vienna we even danced under the stars to a live orchestra. One of the most interesting people I remember from our visit to Austria was our local tour guide, a Rumanian, named Josef Adam, who gave us a very interesting lesson on how we should appreciate the United States of America. He told of some of the atrocities that we in the US only read about in the newspaper or see on TV. This guide also happened to be seated next to me at dinner that evening and even though he spoke broken English, he was an interesting person to listen to. He had a passion for freedom and certainly wanted to remind all of us what a precious commodity we have...living in freedom!!

The last stop on our European trip was in Rome, Italy. As had been the constant through our trip was the good and the bad. Maybe I was just getting tired and ready to go home but we were really missing our kids, but there was so much to see and do in Rome. The one that did me in was the trip to the catacombs. I had to take a taxi back to the hotel and try to restructure my digestive system. I think I had become overly saturated with 'culture', and to really let me know I was ready to go home. But before we left for the good ole USA we were taken to the home of a family that treated us as though we were family. I even corresponded with one of the daughters, Maria Fiumi, for about a year after we returned home. They also had a daughter who was about the same age as our 15 year old. Her name was Lorenzo. One would think that new ideas would not be forthcoming, but again we were surprised and treated to homemade champagne and watermelon, served in the backyard of their home…not too unlike a family reunion. The one thing I remember wanting so badly that I was trying to figure out how I could call ahead to the airport in New York and have ready a huge SALAD. Salads were just not served the entire trip. Since we couldn't make arrangements ahead of time, we settled for a lounge in the airport to chow down on a good salad full of those luscious greens!!

As this all happened around our wedding anniversary and my birthday was also coming up shortly, the kids insisted that they all meet us at our house for yet another surprise! This was 2 am, Gail and I were both so tired we felt like we just might sleep for a couple of days, but we humored the kids and met our surprise! We got a new puppy. We named him Merf! He was a coal black peek-a-poo and only six weeks old and could fit in the palm of my hand. It was worth the extra time to get to spend with our kids, and I think they missed us as much as we had missed them. But here we are back home and ready to jump back into a routine!

As to the recognition I mentioned that belonged to President Eisenhower, he instigated the Interstate highway system, a system that we have become so used to that we hardly remember when it wasn't there. President Dwight David Eisenhower had already made a name for himself in the military. He was a retired five star general, who, along with his team members made the plans for the invasion of

Normandy Beach in France, in June 6, 1945, 'D-Day' a daring feat that was the predecessor to the defeat of Nazi Germany and Adolph Hitler, eventually leading to what was termed 'V-E' Day, bringing an end to the war in Europe followed soon by the defeat of the Japanese in August 1945, known as V-J Day. Finally there was an end to a terrible war that changed our nation, and the world forever!

6 pictures of various stages of Witte Milling Company

The real glue, other than God Himself, that has held this family together is the business that has served three generations of our family.

119

The patriarch of our family was a man named Ernest Henry (Jake) Witte, who purchased the feed mill from the Wallace family in 1930 for $5,000.00. The mill changed as was necessary with the times, from manufacturing flour and corn meal, to most any variety of feeds an animal might need, using their own grains and mixed to each ones specification. When prepared mixes came on the market, there was less need for flour, so realizing the little small town mill could not compete with the big corporations, the mill no longer manufactured flour. It wasn't too long that cornbread mixes also made a big dent in the cornmeal sales, there had to be other changes made. It seems that whatever door closed another opened and the mill began storing, cleaning and selling grain, especially wheat, corn and soybeans. Semi-trucks were purchased, and storage tanks were built as well as a method of cleaning, especially the wheat and soybeans.

As the changes were being made here, there were also changes in the management. Jake's son Gail, who became my husband joined his father in promoting the growing business. Gail came aboard as a partner in 1945, a year after he graduated college and finished his military service in the Naval Air Force. It wasn't until 1950 that I met Gail and we were married. In 1969 Jake had a heart attack that he took seriously enough that he felt he should give Gail more say in the business and Gail then became manager and owner. But Jake came to the mill every day and did what he could.

In 1974 Jake was out helping a customer unload some grain, when he came into the office not looking too well. He sat in a chair, and we all realized he was in trouble. I went to attend to him while Gail called for an ambulance, hoping we could get Jake to the hospital.

As I was at Jake's side, I asked about his nitro glycerin pills I knew he kept in his pants pocket. But all he could say was that he wanted to lie down. The only thing to accommodate him was the office floor. I slowly lowered him down and rested his head on my lap as I searched his pockets for his heart pills and we waited for the ambulance. Things did not look good, and I could not hold back the tears as I had the feeling we were losing a wonderful man. By the time the ambulance came the news was that there was no need to take him to the hospital...he had already left us to meet his Lord! Granddaughter

Vikki, our oldest child, wrote about him. At least our children were privileged to know and love a man they affectionately called "Popo". Here is Vikki's tribute to a great man:

ONE CALLED HIM HONEY

Winter has come and his work is done
Although we hate to see him go
For he loved the Son and helped everyone
And you know we all loved him so.

One called him honey
Two called him daddy
Three called him grandpa
But most folks called him Jake.

He knew no fear, to God he was near
He stood by to watch us grow.
He was so dear to everyone here,
And when we saw him how his eyes would glow.

One called him honey,
Two called him daddy
Three called him grandpa,
But most folks called him Jake.

But his time has passed he's with Him at last
A journey sometimes hard to make.
Our tears will pass and our love will last
For part of us with him did he take.

One called him honey
Two called him daddy
Three called him grandpa,
But most folks called him Jake.

January 24, 1974
By Vikki Bishop

This is a wonderful, heartfelt gift from her young heart that expressed all our feelings!

One person I never got to meet but would love to have had that privilege...it was Jake Witte's mother...Gail's grandmother. She passed away in 1948 and I didn't come to Dale until 1949. Her name was Elizabeth and at age 16 she stowed away on a ship from Bremen, Germany along with her younger mentally retarded brother. It was during the 1930's with Hitler's rise to power in Germany and Grandma Witte knew her brother would not survive the Germany she saw coming. It was amazing enough that this young girl took it upon herself to try to save her brother, but I have never been told how the Witte clan found its way to Perry County, Indiana before moving to Dale. All I know of this is tid-bits of stories told to me, and I believe I missed meeting a wonderful woman.

'Remember When'...

Pics of choice of Mill

Wallace / Mitte Mill - Dale, Indiana   1847 - 1994

3 Dale Witte Milling Company operated by E. H. Witte, was originally the old Wallace Mill. Mr. Witte has owned the company now since 1936. Left to right are: Ed Schum, packer, Clarence Elliott, miller, Gail Witte and E. H. Witte. The firm which manufactures flour and feeds has a capacity of 50 barrels a day.

As it came Gails' turn to totally run the business, he had a remarkable foreman in Jim VanWinkle, a man who could practically make something out of nothing. We were beginning to realize that the days of the small town feed mill would soon fade as many other businesses have done. While Gail was looking for a buyer and his retirement, Jim held the mill parts together *with bailing wire and chewing gum*, so Gail liked to say. This was Gail's analysis of how we were hanging on. Of course there was a need for a secretary in such an office, and Jake's wife Booty was there for many years. Then the need grew and 2 office girls were required. Each of our kids were given an opportunity, but none felt it their calling to work full time at the mill. After our children were grown, I worked the office and really enjoyed it. But again we knew there needed to be someone else, also, and we hired Jim's, daughter Angie. Talk about efficient and loyal, Angie was top of the list.

I just have to interject a funny story that happened to one of our employees. When I worked in the office, I saw that the men got hungry mid-morning and I started a coffee shop and bought or brought from home something I felt they would enjoy. A pot of Chili on a cold, snowy morning sure felt good to their stomachs. Living in a German community also meant turtle soup! It seemed every family sported their recipe. This turtle soup is not made with real turtle, but rather beef and chicken (I think). So one day I proudly brought my steaming pot of turtle soup. We had an employee named Kenny Elverd, and when snack time came Kenny came anxiously down the stairs from the feed room to get his treat. Seeing the soup pot, Kenny asked what was in it, and when I said 'turtle soup', I have never seen anyone do an about face and retreat back up the stairs any faster than Kenny Elverd, never to be seen in the office anymore until time to check out that day after work. I think it is safe to say Kenny did not like turtle soup even though he probably had never tasted it. Anyway, we had a good laugh from that.

Another true happening that we were told by one of the farmers who 'knew everything'! It seems that one of the farmers, Joe Hassfurther, evidently thought I was pretty enough to talk about. So he asked his farmer friends: "Have you been to the mill since Gail's wife started working? She's so pretty it would make you want to buy a bag of hog feed even if you didn't have a hog!" Now that is what I would call a real compliment!

We had customers I could write another book about. They were priceless farmers, some good humored and some with a forever chip on their shoulder, but never one I could not get a smile out of by the time they left. The aroma often left by the hog farmers had to be treated with a can of spray, but their loyalty and friendship will never be forgotten.

For part of our chance to 'get away', Gail and I purchased a 'Time-Share' in Tennessee. We went there for the first week in April each year. We loved it down there. We played golf and invited friends to visit. It was not far away and yet we could relax and unwind a bit from the stress of business life...but one morning...April 17, 1994...our telephone rang at 2am. This is NEVER good, and it wasn't! Our daughter Sarah called to tell us that our MILL WAS ON FIRE!! Anyone who knows about small town grain elevators knows they are mainly old and made of wood surrounded by grain dust, but in this case it was a tank of fat what was kept hot. We kept the liquid hot to be put on certain feeds. And the belief was that there had either been a leak in the tank or an electrical shortage that caused the fire.

Our Time-Share was 5 hours away and it was one of the quietest rides home I can remember. I feel sure Gail's mind was running somewhat like mine, but for different reasons. Mainly, our thoughts were: "Just what will we find when we get there?"

When we arrived back in Dale, not surprisingly, Gail went straight to the charred remains of what had been our life's blood...me...I saw a local pastor whom I also knew as a friend, and I needed someone to just let me cry on, and he did!

Some of the firemen were still there when we arrived. What a job they had done!! The local fire chief told us that this particular building was what the area departments all practiced for. They knew it would be the really big one since these structures are prime targets for fires. We were thankful that the fire happened the time of night that it did. It meant our employees were not bodily harmed. I believe in all, there were five area fire departments at the scene. They had contained the fire so well I couldn't help but notice that where we had placed half car tires over the coverings of the portholes in our big steel grain bin to protect the customers from harming their vehicles...those tires were in very close proximity to the mill office, yet they we not damaged a bit.

But the fire burned from about midnight until daybreak and beyond. Gail and I arrived at the scene about 9:30 am, and were told the fire was sighted by two student monks from St. Meinrad, who had come into town for a snack a Circle S. Virgil Heneisen, the local fire chief, was reported to have said that there were 70 firefighters on the scene that had flames shooting into the sky over 100 feet and was visible in Huntingburg, a town 8 miles away. I truly believe that what remained can only be credited to the magnificent group of fire fighters at a time of our town's real need!!

When the shock wore off a bit, Gail realized that after he got the mess cleaned up from the fire, he could start working on his retirement. God seems to take care of things and that is the only way we looked at this tragedy. We still had out buildings and a big prime corner lot. This happening in April gave Gail time to do whatever he had to do to clean up, but still left us with buildings and property.

Fortunately, as is seemingly always the way things go, things just have a way of working out. Kenny Neighbors who had married our daughter Sarah had an interest in keeping the mill running and we had already begun receiving calls from former customers expressing the need for this little feed mill to continue.

The mill building itself was built in 1847 and in the 1970's we were given recognition from the state of Indiana for having a business in continual operation for 100+ years.

The summer was filled with cleaning, planning and wondering just what we would do.

Gail had often said he wanted to keep a little table saw that was in one of the garages at the mill. This was the beginning of a joy-filled retirement for him. He eventually became quite a good wood craftsman as I have mentioned.

Next we started planning a retirement dinner for Gail. Office and management personnel, family and friends gathered at our favorite place, "The Log Inn" in Warrenton, IN on a Saturday evening in late August…but this was not the end of Witte Milling Company. Our son-in-law was among those without a job as a result of the fire. He had told Gail that he felt he could make a go of a business on a lesser scale.

So in just a few days after the retirement dinner, the doors were opened on Witte Feeds. Gail invested the insurance money into equipment for Kenny, and it is still in operation today in October, 2019! Still a continuing business leased from Witte Milling Company. Kenny & Sarah made this their business by incorporating as Witte Feeds, Inc.. Angie, our wonderful office girl stayed with us as secretary until I moved to Evansville, in 2015. She was the *best*! The scary moment for me came in 2008, shortly before Gail passed away when he asked me to take over as president of the company. I told him I wasn't sure I was up to the job. He assured me I was and here I am today Still hanging in there, as president *and* secretary and wondering when, if ever, I will get to retire! Three generations still going on a wonderful business!

It seems I have traversed time and the globe in relating some things that started out as information and fun for my children grandchildren and great-grandchildren, but along the way I found more people interested in life as I remember it, and have come up with a group of stories that I hope will stir people's hearts and memories…back to a time that was and never will be again. Along the way you have witnessed some of my personal struggles but hopefully I have conveyed the part that my faith in my Lord and Savior, Jesus Christ has been in every day of it whether it was a good day or a not so good day. In bringing it to a close, I can think of no better way that to share with you a story that, our daughter Sarah Neighbors wrote at a time when they were certain several times that I would not be with them very long. But that was 12 years ago and is the family's desire to not have those few days fade from memory. Sarah wrote about all of the events she and my family experienced while my life was literally hanging in the balance. I have been granted permission to print the story here and I find no better way to put an exclamation point to my life. Enjoy it and share it, for it is only by the grace of God that I am here today.

Mom's Story

We were on our way to the ER (Memorial Hospital, Jasper, IN), again! This was the fourth time in the last five days, each time adding another complication to the list of problems. First there was the weight gain of more than 40 pounds in about a six week period, followed by leg cramping and body jerks, complicated breathing and now confusion and lethargy. What could be next?

About 2:30 pm on Tuesday, April 3, 2007, I pulled into the ER. I had always taken Mom in by myself, but this time I was going to need assistance. The emt's quickly came to my aid and escorted my Mom into the usual little room for a quick check in and then off to the exam room. They had always been very professional and helpful, but this time seemed different. The attention they were giving seemed very focused.

They started an IV, inserted a catheter, asked questions, drew blood and sent her off to radiology for a CT scan and Xrays. I couldn't help wondering if they would finally keep her in the hospital. I was hoping they would as I was running out of ideas on what to do for her.

I watched the news. There was a severe thunderstorm coming and I had to leave my Dad at home alone. I didn't worry, though, I knew God was watching over him.

In just a few moments, I heard over the intercom, "Code blue! All personnel-Code blue!" I wondered if there had been an accident and I expected an ambulance to drive in at any moment. Everyone was scattering. I kept thinking, "I wish Mom would get back. That way I will know it's not her."

After about 30 minutes, a nurse came to my room and said, "Are you Mrs. Witte's daughter?"

"Yes," I answered.

"Are you alone?"

"Yes."

Then she said, "Your Mom is very sick and I need to ask what your wishes are for life support."

It was like someone had just turned on a faucet as I began to cry.

The nurse quickly escorted me to a counseling room. I asked if I needed to call my family to the hospital and he answered, "Yes."

I called my husband and told him I needed him to come to the hospital and that he needed to let everyone else in the family know they also needed to come. He said, "I'll be right there."

The 'on-call doctor and the nurse all met with me. They said that Mom had a massive heart attack while they were drawing blood. It took them about two minutes to revive her and she was vomiting violently. Her liver was damaged and her kidneys had shut down. They had her hooked to life support and were taking her to ICU.

The nurse escorted me to the ICU waiting room and asked if there was anything I needed. I asked to get to the phones to make another call. I kept trying to call out, but I couldn't seem to get the phones to work. This could be because of the severe storms in the area. Besides that, my cell phone battery was dead.

We finally found a phone that would work in the nurse's station. I called Judy Walton. She prayed with me over the phone and started a prayer chain after hearing the news. My brother, sister and Dad all put Mom on the prayer chains at their respective churches as well, Christian Fellowship Church, Bethel Temple and Redeemer Lutheran churches, all in Evansville, and Dale Bible church in Dale. My daughter Autumn called our Bible study group which meets on Tuesday nights. They met early to pray for Mom that night and also prayed again after the Bible study was over.

It seemed like an eternity as I sat there waiting. Then the heart doctor came in to speak to me. He was the specialist that had been assigned to Mom! He is an incredible doctor!

He told me that my Mom was very sick and that she was in liver failure, kidney failure, had a massive heart attack and was on life support. Then he asked a series on questions about her health which I answered to the best of my ability:

She has type II diabetes; she has skin cancer (some of which have been removed surgically from one leg, but wasn't healing; the other leg had several spots yet to be removed; she has been overweight for years; she is on enough medication to choke a horse, (I handed him the list of medications).

He asked what our wishes were in regard to life support. I told him to only use life support as a means to bring her back to a 'functioning' life, but not as a way of life.

He asked about dialysis. I told him that we could do that.

He said he would do everything he could to help my Mom, but it didn't look very good. I told him to just do his best!

I just sat there a while. My body felt numb. I almost couldn't feel anything. I was upset and wanted my family to be with me, but I also had a peace in my heart.

One of our church elders arrived. I was glad to see a familiar face. He asked how I was doing. I thought I was a mess, but he said I appeared to be doing better that he had expected. We talked a while and then the pastor from Dale Bible church came, as well as my family.

We all sat around trying to comfort one another and feeling like this wasn't really happening. My brother, Rick, said to me, "If you were in her place and you could either die and be with the Lord, or come back to life on Earth, what would you rather do?"

I really appreciated that because I knew that I would choose to be with the Lord. It made me realize that I would be selfish to ask God to let her stay.

My sister, Vikki, and I went back to see Mom in ICU. We held hands and prayed that God would do whatever He felt would bring Him the most Glory. We called for my Dad and brother as we all held hands and stood with her around the room. We said what we wanted to say to her.

Dad thanked her for the 56 years of marriage. We told her we understood if she wanted to go, but we would still like her to stay with us, grim as it was. We all believed that her next breath very well could be her last, but we were ready to let her go if it was God's will. It was a precious time!

As the evening went along, everyone except my daughter, Elana, and I went home. The hospital gave us a comfort room which was like a hotel room. It had beds, a private bath and TV. It was right across from Mom's room. They couldn't have treated us better.

When Elana's husband, Justin, got off work at midnight, he came to the hospital and joined us. He slept on the floor and Elana and I slept in the beds. I never did sleep. I remember lying in bed thinking that I really should go to Mom's room and check to see how she was doing. But I just lay there thinking and hoping maybe I would fall asleep.

Just then I heard that same call over the intercom-"Code blue"- I immediately jumped up. I knew it was Mom. I opened the door to the hall and the nurse was rounding the corner and waving for me to come. I tapped Elana on the leg and said, "It's Mom, we have to go." Then I ran down the hall. Once again she was in full cardiac arrest.

Her room was filled with doctors and nurses. Mom's nurse was on the phone to the specialist. He was giving orders and the nurse was calling them out to the team. It was a sight to behold!

I just stood there with Elana holding me as I cried. I told Elana that part of me wants to let her go. I wondered if I should just tell them to stop and let her pass. I didn't want to bring her back just to do this all over again.

I walked to the doorway where I could see her face. It was still and lifeless. Something inside me said, "Just wait."

It seemed like an hour, but it was really only five minutes. Then I heard someone say, "I have a pulse."

I was sick and crying and hurting inside. But at the same time I had a peace that was soothing my very soul.

Elana and I spent the rest of the night beside her bed holding her hand. Elana was on one side and I on the other. We just talked to Mom. Elana asked her if she wanted us to let her go. She said, "yes."

My heart just ached at the thought. I wanted to be absolutely sure because she could only communicate by a hand squeeze. I wondered if this had been a reflex because of the body jerks, or if this was real and deliberate.

We asked her again and her response confirmed that she wanted to go.

I knew I was her Power of Attorney, and had in my hand her Living Will. I could do this and end this for her, but I could not! Nothing in me would let me carry this out. I told Elana that we needed to pray that if God wanted her to go He would have to take her because I just couldn't let her go. So we prayed.

We were in the waiting room when the nurse came in with the news that her organs were beginning to respond and she was actually producing some urine on her own. We immediately went to her bed and told her how well she was doing and that we were so proud of her. So we asked her if she wanted to stay and fight and she definitely responded, "Yes."

What a relief!!

Early the next morning, I called home to give a progress report about the second heart attack and the turn around. Everyone was surprised and we began to think of a recovery instead of a funeral, but she had only turned the first corner. She was still very sick. The doctor said things were looking better and they would continue to work with her, because she was not out of the woods yet.

Mom's nephew, Jeff Spalding, arrived from Indianapolis about noon and was pleased to hear of her change. So were the other visitors who stopped in- all friends from the various churches.

As evening came so did more prayers. Three of the men from our Tuesday night Bible study group came to the hospital. They knew the Lord was leading them to come as a group to pray for Mom.

Dan, Charlie, Tony, Autumn and I all sat in the ICU waiting room and prayed for everyone on the floor. I told them that Mom was having a hard time relaxing and I really wanted to pray for her to be able to rest. She hadn't seemed to rest at all-even though she was unconscious, her body jerked continuously. She was unable to receive any pain medication because her blood pressure was so low -at times not even registering.

Her mouth was dry from the tubes and stomach pump. They were also pumping out her lungs because she had developed pneumonia in her right lung from the vomiting after her first 'code blue'. She wanted a drink so badly and the only thing we could do was run a tiny sponge over her lips and tongue.

She kept improving and became more alert and aware of her pain. The jerking was so bad they had to use mild wrist restraints to keep her from pulling out the tubes and IV's.

We gathered in her room to pray- Jeff, Autumn, Tony, Charlie, Elana and me. We encircled the bed and held hands as we began to pray. The Holy Spirit was invited in and our requests were made known to the Lord as we prayed for healing. We prayed specifically for her kidneys, liver and blood pressure and praised God for Who He is.

His presence was definitely in that room!

After praying, the men left and one of the nurses came to me. I knew she was struggling with something that evening. She said she was so upset because her brother had a heart attack on Monday and was in a hospital in Virginia. He wanted her to talk to his nurse in the hospital he was in, but they were so busy she didn't have time. I asked her what his name was and she replied, "Scott." I told her I would call the prayer team and we would pray for Scott. She was so thankful.

The next morning, on Thursday, I called Dad to give him an update on Mom. Before I could speak he said, "I have to tell you what I dreamed last night."

He said: "I dreamed there was a group of people who gathered together in Mom's room and they all held hands and were praying over her." Then he said that God spoke to him and said not to worry, that He was in complete control and that Elana and Sarah were the stars of the show, because they had not left her side. I told him that except for the idea about the 'stars of the show', it was NOT a dream-it was a vision of exactly what happened!

From that day on Mom improved so quickly. All of her organs

began to function normally. No dialysis was necessary and her liver was healing. I knew in my heart we had experienced a miracle from God!

The doctor had originally told us that after about a week in ICU, Mom would be facing about a month in the regular recovery room, followed by another month in rehab. On Saturday, on only her fifth day in the ICU, she was taken off life support and began to talk and eat and said she felt the inside of her was like a newborn baby and she was overwhelmed!

I know that in everything there is a lesson and a blessing. We have received many blessings from this, but what I have learned in a very powerful way is the power of prayer. When you spend 5 days in ICU, you can see a lot. There are many who claim to be Christian and yet will speak of prayer as a last resort. What I have learned is that, for the believer who knows and has a personal relationship with Almighty God, through Jesus Christ...Prayer is our first line of defense.

Since then we have heard that one of the hospital staff on the floor that night had been suffering from a bad hip. She had been in a lot of pain, but the night we prayed for Mom, her pain went away and has not returned.

I later found out that there was a woman in the room next to Mom who had been on life support for several days without response. On Wednesday the doctor told the family there was no hope and they made that very difficult decision to turn off her life support. The family gathered together waiting for her to pass away.

Sometime early Thursday morning she sat up and asked for something to eat. She had been healed and was well!

I will never underestimate the power of prayer and what God can do!

Prepared by
Sarah Neighbors, 2007
With eternal thanks to my Lord and Savior, Jesus Christ

(These are just pictures of interest that I felt should add to the book)

Aunt Nellie, Aunt Bettie and Mother

Our son Rick Witte, wife Regina, Jake and Galina

Jean, ready for the next show?

Sarah, the apprentice wood crafter, under the watchful eyes of her dad

Our family at Christmas 2018:

Waiting line. From door: Jean, Sarah, Gail, Vikki & Regina.
Colorada Dude Ranch August, 1997.

Dorothy, my 15 year old sister
holding me just a few months old.

Epilogue

J ean *(my mother)* had her fair share of hardship, although she never saw herself as a victim or unfortunate in any way. She delt with a lot of pain and other physical issues during her lifetime, but never lost her faith. She always knew there was a reason for her suffering. She gracefully embraced whatever her Lord handed her and never lost her joy.

It was a dream of hers to write and publish a book, however she was only able to accomplish part of that dream. My precious mother passed away on October 11, 2020 before her book was published. I made a promise to her the day she left for her heavenly home that I would see to it her book was published at last.

It is my pleasure to offer this tribute to one of the most wonderful people that ever graced the planet. Here's to you mom. I love you, Sarah.

Printed in the United States
by Baker & Taylor Publisher Services